The Register of Free Negroes

Northampton County
Virginia

1853 to 1861

Transcribed, Referenced
and Indexed

by

Frances Bibbins Latimer

HERITAGE BOOKS
2012

HERITAGE BOOKS
AN IMPRINT OF HERITAGE BOOKS, INC.

Books, CDs, and more—Worldwide

For our listing of thousands of titles see our website
at
www.HeritageBooks.com

Published 2012 by
HERITAGE BOOKS, INC.
Publishing Division
100 Railroad Ave. #104
Westminster, Maryland 21157

Copyright © 1992 Frances Bibbins Latimer

Other Heritage Books by the author:
1860 Census for Northampton County, Virginia
1870 Census for Northampton County, Virginia
An Original List of Taxable Property within the County of Northampton, Virginia 1796
Instruments of Freedom: Deeds and Wills of Emancipation, Northampton County, Virginia, 1782-1864
Register of Free Negroes and Certificates of Freedom, Northampton County, Virginia, 1793-1864
Remembering Cape Charles: A Place for All People
Robert S. Costin of Northampton County, Virginia: Claims of a Loyal Citizen for Supplies Furnished During the Rebellion, Claim #55231
The Register of Free Negroes, Northampton County, Virginia, 1853-1861

All rights reserved. No part of this book may be reproduced or transmitted in any form or by any means, electronic or mechanical, including photocopying, recording or by any information storage and retrieval system without written permission from the author, except for the inclusion of brief quotations in a review.

International Standard Book Numbers
Paperbound: 978-1-55613-622-1
Clothbound: 978-0-7884-9226-6

TABLE OF CONTENTS

	PAGE
ACKNOWLEDGMENT	v
PREFACE	vii
FOOTNOTES	xv
NOTES ON THE REGISTER OF FREE NEGROES	xvii
GUIDE TO AFRICAN AMERICAN SURNAMES	xix
ILLUSTRATION OF ORIGINAL REGISTER	xxii
THE REGISTER OF FREE NEGROES	1
APPENDIX I	
Example of Free Negro Certification	45
APPENDIX II	
Notes on Wills and Virginia Laws	47
Relevant Virginia Laws (1639-1861)	48
APPENDIX III	
Notes on the Wills	61
Wills of Emancipation	62
APPENDIX IV	
Definition of Legal Terms	69
REFERENCES	73
INDEX OF FREE NEGROES	75

ACKNOWLEDGMENT

It is impossible for me to write about the Eastern Shore of Virginia without it being personal to me. It is impossible for me to read the records and touch the old deeds and wills without being emotional. This is the place where family and friends live; even in the old records of the "Shore" there are family and friends. This is home.

Symbolic of the "Shore", I met and was helped by new friends in transcribing the *Register of Free Negroes*. Estelle Murphy and Mary Linda Elliot of the Northampton County Clerk's Office, under the direction of Mr. Kenneth Arnold, are two such people. They were never too busy; always eager to answer questions. Jean Mihalyka comes under the category of help when help is needed. The "Shore" is their home, too.

I wish to acknowledge the help of Ms. Susie C. Bowles and Ms. Margaret M. Carpenter of Register of Wills Office in Charles County, Maryland. This department was instrumental in securing for me the Simon Wilmer Will.

In the tradition of the Eastern Shore of Virginia, but not of the "Shore", I wish to acknowledge Marty Blaustein and Kevin McManus. The willingness of these gentlemen to share their knowledge of computers and expertise in typesetting helped me to finish this project.

Mr. John R. Collins, Jr. was a special help. In the *Register of Free Negroes* I found his paternal great-grandparents. Both Mr. and Mrs. Collins have always taken the time to tell me about this person or that person. Over the years they have helped me to discover the "Shore" through their eyes.

Kirsten Bibbins is my niece. She studied two years at the University of Ibadan in Nigeria, West Africa and has traveled there since she returned to this country. Her insights into the African culture was of invaluable importance to me. Her knowledge of Spanish/Portuguese slave trade in Nigeria helped me to better understand the presence of Spanish and Portuguese names in a developing Virginia.

Mr. Gboyega Domingo, a Nigerian gentleman, related stories to my niece about how his family was effected by Spanish/Portuguese slave trade. His first hand knowledge of this subject was instrumental in helping me formulate a theory of how the Eastern Shore of Virginia fitted into the total picture of African slave trade.

With the aid of my parents, Paul and Lillie Bibbins, I found two sets of great-great-grandparents and one set of great-great-great grandparents in the Register of Free Negroes. My mother and father over the years have spent many hours showing me old buildings and remembering with me who had lived there. We have talked about this family member or that church member long dead, but remembered for some special reason. And sometimes not remembered, "just heard of".

Last, but not least, I wish to acknowledge my husband, George, whose understanding of how close my ties are to the Eastern Shore allowed me to do the transcription and the research necessary to finish this book.

February, 1992

Frances Bibbins Latimer
Bloxom, Virginia

PREFACE

The contents of this book have been transcribed from the original manuscript of *The Register of Free Negroes, Northampton County, Virginia-1853-1861*. The original manuscript is on file in the Northampton County Clerk's Office in Eastville, Virginia. The County seat of Eastville on the Eastern Shore of Virginia is reputed for having the longest continuous historical record in the United States. Northampton County was the first area on the peninsula to be settled; although at that time the settlers called it Accomack. On July 28, 1643, the name was changed to Northampton. Twenty years after the area was renamed, it was divided by population rather than geography into two counties: Northampton to the south, and Accomack to the north. In 1670 Northampton and Accomack were reunited into a single county. In 1673 the two counties were divided again.

When the Eastern Shore of Virginia was settled, most of the people coming into the colony were "in bondage." White people were indentured servants and the first Africans were transported to Virginia from the West Indies as slaves. The English were sometimes escaping debts and very often serving time for crimes. They were brought here to serve out that time. The Africans on the other hand were brought here to work. Beverly in 1705 made the distinction between indentured servitude and slavery when he said, " They are call'd slaves in respect of the time of their servitude, because it is for life.",

During this time of the development of slavery in Virginia, who were the free Negroes and how did they become free? Who are the people who are registered in this book? There were three legally accepted ways of manumission in the state of Virginia: (1) by an act of the legislature, (2) by last will and testament, and (3) by deed. The free Negroes registered here were freed by wills of their deceased masters, freed by deeds of emancipation and those whose families had been servants for life, but freed through hard work. Many of the families represented in this book were families who reached freedom before the loss of liberty was made complete by slavery of the late seventeenth century.

The officials of Northampton County instituted the use of this particular register in 1853 as a result of the passing of several acts in the General Assembly and a changing of attitudes toward free Negroes which led to a very uneasy coexistence between free Negroes and slave owners. Prior to the use of this register, free Negroes were certified in court. In these certification actions there were no descriptions kept. A sample of a" certifying of free Negroes" may be seen in Appendix I. In 1831 a law was passed making it mandatory that all registered free negroes be described in detail. I cannot account for the nineteen years that Northampton County did not have a detailed Register of Free Negroes. It is possible that there is an older Register of Free Negroes that has not been discovered or that it has been destroyed. The possibility also exists that after the laws were passed to remove free Negroes from Northampton County there were so few free Negroes that a formal register was not needed. Overcome by curiosity, recently I inquired at the Accomack County Clerk's Office about a Register of Free Negroes for Accomack County. I was told that the Clerk's Office did not house such a book. Those working in that office did not think that one ever existed.

An overview of the events which led to the institution of *The Register of Free Negroes* is needed to explore and understand the dynamics involved in slavery and the condition of freedom generally in the state of Virginia and specifically on the Eastern Shore of Virginia.

During the first forty years of the settling of the Eastern Shore of Virginia, African immigrants were loosely held as slaves. They served their masters and were very often able to purchase their freedom through additional work. After they reached freedom, they were able to acquire land, marry, have families and live an existence not unlike the freed white indentured servant. There is evidence, however, that the free African's position in the community was precarious.

In doing the research for this book, I came across two opinions with reference to how early slavery began and if Africans were first endentured servants and then slaves. There is evidence that the problem in determining whether there was slavery during the beginning years of Virginia is a problem of semantics. The Africans were referred to as servants. The first laws to effect Africans referred to them as negroes. Some twenty years after the first law effecting Africans was passed, the Virginia General Assembly began referring to Africans as slaves.

The early records of the Northampton County show clearly that these servants were held for life. In Ames' transcription of *County Court Records Northampton-Accomack, Virginia, 1640-1645* Nathaniel Littleton freed his servant, Antony Longgee (Longoe). "To All to whome these presentes shall come greetings in our Lord [god everlastinge]. Know yee that whereas Antony Longee the Negro beinge [formerly] my servant and soly and propperly belongeing unto mee [Nathaniel Litt]leton of Accomack in the Colony ov Virginia Esquire And allsoe whereas I the said Nathaniel Littleton haveing Formerly viz. in the yeare of our Lord god one thousand six hundred thirty and Five and one the sixteenth day of March in the same yeare by a certen wrytinge under my hand dated as afforesaid really and Freely acquitted discharged released and set Free him the said Anthony Longoe From all service and servitude whatsoever from the Beginning of the World untill that present day viz. the sixteenth day of March above specified Nowe Knowe yee that I the said nathaniell Littleton in confirmation of my aforesaid deed in wrytinge expressed and for the certen considerations mee thereunto moveinge doe hereby as my acte and deede doe hereby for mee my heires and assignes, in like manner acquit and discharge release exonerate and Free him the said Antony Longo from all and all of obligementes or dutyes thereupon depending or formerly due even from the beginninge of the World untill this present day without anie Fraud or mentall reservation provisoe contradiction or anie other exception whatsoever thereof as my absolute act and deed at the humble request of him the said Antony Longoe I have hereunto put my hand this thirtyeth day of July Anno Domini 1640. And in the sixteenth yeare of the raigne of our Soveraigne Lord Charles by the grace of god of England Scotland France and Ireland Kinge defender of the Fayth etc." It was signed by Nathaniel Littleton and witnessed by George Dawe. [2]

On the 13th of November 1643 an inventory was taken " of the goods Cattles and Chattles of and belonging unto the state of Mr. William Burdett deceased.......

The servants	pound tob.
Mary Vaughan haveing Eleaven monthes to serve at.........	0400
Sarah Hickman to serve one yeare at.........	0700
John Gibbins to serve one yeare at.........	0650
Nehemia Coventon Aged 12 yeares to 8 yeares at	1000
Symon Caldron a boy very Lame and 14 yeares old to serve 7	0500
William Young another boy full of the scurvey to serve sixe yeares at.........	0600
Edward Southerne a little Boy very sicke haveing seaven yeares to serve at.........	0700
Michaell Pacey a boy to serve sixe yeares at.........	1100
Caine the negro, very anncient at.........	3000
One negro girle about 8 yeares old at.........	2000

[3]

This trancription from *County Court Records of Northampton-Accomack, Virginia 1640-1645* by Susie Ames shows us which are the indentured servants and which are the Negro slaves, although they are called servants. The entries of indentured servants shows the time remaining to serve. The Negro entries show no time because their servitude is for life. Here are two examples of the word servant used to describe people held in bondage for life.

There are other examples of "servants" being freed. There are examples of "servants" purchasing their freedom and that of their families. Anthony Johnson purchased his freedom and went on to become a wealthy land owner. Francis Payne (Paine) and Emanuell Rodriggus both purchased their freedom and became substantial property holders. In some instances the white settler used the term "my Negro." The argument about whether or not the English felt that the African was a slave or a servant is rhetorical; the African was transported from Africa into the colony against his will. If we are to believe that the Africans were slaves from the beginning, it was without laws and by custom.

The examples of Anthony Johnson, Emanuell Rodriggus and Francis Payne are ones we look at curiously in the light of what slavery became less than a generation after these men were freed. It is at this point that we must ask how could these Africans prosper and a generation later there was total poverty for the free African immigrant and complete devastation of the imported African culture? The original Africans had not come directly from Africa. They had learned the ways of the settlers in the West Indies. They knew the language and knew how to move about within a non African system. In the years following Bacon's Rebellion the English planters were able to buy more Africans. The newly purchased Africans came directly from Africa, unprepared and unaccustomed to the ways of the New World. These Africans, newly from Africa, were at the mercy of the English.

As the black population grew those African immigrants, who had purchased their freedom and had prospered as farmers and planters lost favor. The decade between 1660 and 1670 was a time of discovery for the English settlers. What did they want this new world to yield to them? The goals of the English became more clearly defined. Their goal was to live life as "landed gentry". Many of the English settlers were not from elite English families. They wanted all that England could not give them: land, wealth, prosperity and an easy life. None of these goals could be achieved without land and the hands to work that land. Dependable free labor would be an essential part of the growth and development of the "Shore." Indentured servants and a few Africans slaves had served the developing colony, but they were not dependable over a long period of time. The indentured servants worked for a specified number of years and the Africans worked for freedom. A work force was needed that would always be ready to work, a work force that would not want to move or have a holiday, a work force who would not have freedom as a goal, a work force whose will was that of their master.

And so at the beginning of the settlement of the Eastern Shore as in the settlement of the mainland of Virginia there were four distinct and recognizable groups: (1) the English Settlers, (2) poor white people escaping debts and crime, (3) Indian American natives, and (4) Africans brought here against their will.

The move to discard indentured servitude and have slavery as the only method to supply the work force was relatively simple. There were Indians, Africans and poor white people from which to choose. As it turned out Indians held as slaves succumbed to excessive labor and diseases brought to the new world by white people. Landless whites proved to be unsuitable because of their ability to disappear into the white population; importing more African slaves was the best option. Furthermore, the English had used the Africans as slaves in the West Indies. Indeed many of the Africans coming into the new World had been slaves in the West Indies. The institution of slavery was well established in the West Indies by 1640.

The Africans that were already in the colony and had through work reached freedom remained free, but the Africans entering the colony after the 1670's were imported with slave laws in place. Prior to these laws African immigrants were able to seek relief from servitude through working and purchasing freedom. The slave laws added new resolve and purpose. There was no longer the need for peaceful coexistence. The new incoming Africans could not speak English, they were innocent of what was to be their existence.

As time went on many of the families of the first free Negroes moved to Accomack County in the northern part of the Eastern Shore of Virginia and Somerset and Worcester counties in southern Maryland. The new supply of Africans had created a more restrained environment for free African immigrants.

In *Free Negroes in Virginia, 1619-1865*, Russell states that slavery began in Virginia in 1670. The law of 1670 seems to have put a finality to the subject of slavery. On October 3, 1670 it was enacted that "all servants not christians, being imported into this country by shipping shall be slaves for their lives..."[3] We could say that the law of 1670 legalized slavery in Virginia.

The first law in Virginia relating to Africans was passed in 1639. This law made it illegal for a "Negro" to have firearms and ammunitions. In 1630 Hugh Davis was to be "soundly whipped before an assembly of Negroes and other for abusing himself to the dishonor of God and shame of Christians, by defiling his body in lying with a negro;....."[4] In 1640 Robert Sweet was sentenced to do "penance in church according to laws of England, for getting a negro woman with child and the woman whipt."[5] As early as 1659 Africans were referred to as "Negro slaves". There seems to be no time, no date, no day that marked the beginning of slavery. It was always there.

Slowly the practice of slavery moved from slavery by custom to slavery by statute as more laws were passed. The Africans who had worked to be free on the "Shore" during its beginning continued to be free, but legislation continued to be passed that effected these free Negroes as well as slaves. As years of development passed, slavery became more ensconced as a way of supplying a work force; there seemed to be no place for African immigrants except in bondage.

Free Negroes were seen as unnecessary, without obvious function in the development of the colony. They were seen as a threat to the institution of slavery. African slaves were taught that they could not trust free Negroes. In a system that had been created for only two groups, (free white settlers and slaves), the free African walked an uneasy path. The feeling of suspicion toward this anomaly expressed itself in the laws that were passed, in the local and state politics, in the literary writing of the time, and in the day to day treatment of this group of Africans.

Very early in slavery there were dissenting voices, religious voices raised against perpetual bondage of any person. In 1652 a Quaker resolution read as follows:

"Whereas there is a common course practiced among Englishmen, to buy negroes to that end that they may have them for service or as slaves forever; for the preventing of such practices among us, let it be ordered, that no black mankind or white being shall be forced, by covenant, bond, or otherwise, to serve any man or his assignees for longer than ten years...." [6]

In 1688 the Germantown Mennonites protested the institution of slavery at a monthly meeting.

"There are reasons why we are against the traffic of mens-body, as followeth: Is there any that would be done or handled at this manner? viz., to be sold or made a slave for all the time of his life? How fearful and faint-hearted are many at sea, when they see a strange vessel, being afraid it a Turk, and they should be taken, and sold for slaves into Turkey. Now, what is this better done, than Turks do? Yea, rather it is worse for them, which say they are Christians..." [7]

During the late 1700's Methodism began development on the Eastern Shore. This development was significant because one of the tenets of the church was that the preachers of this new denomination as well as its members could not own slaves. At a conference held in Baltimore, Maryland the subject of slavery was addressed in the following manner:

Ought not this conference to require those traveling preachers who hold slaves to give promises to set them free?
Does this conference acknowledge that slavery is contrary to the laws of God, man, and nature, and hurtful to society: contrary to the dictates of conscience and pure religion, and doing that which we would not others should do to us and ours? Do we pass our disapprobation on all our friends who keep slaves, and advise their freedom? [8]

In addition to the influence of the Methodist Church, the southern Quakers added to the trend toward intolerance of slavery by the various religious groups. In 1785 the following question was asked at the Upper Quarterly Meeting: "Do any Friends hold slaves and do all bear a faithful testimony against the practice?"

In 1788 the following statement was inserted in the Friends Discipline: *"none amongst us to be concerned in importing, buying, selling, holding, or overseeing slaves, and that all bear a faithful testimony against the practice."* In 1796 at a meeting of the Friends there was no longer complaints of Friends' holding slaves when they could be lawfully liberated. [9]

In 1782 an Act was passed making it legal for a slave holder to emancipate any slave of his or her choice. As a result of this law Africans long held as slaves were emancipated by deeds and wills and the total number of free Negroes in the state of Virginia increased to a level that made white Virginians uncomfortable. [9]

Fear of having too many free Negroes in one area is the reason for the passage of the Act of 1806. "If any slave hereafter emancipated shall remain within this Commonwealth more than twelve months after his or her right to freedom shall have accrued he or she shall forfeit all such right and may be apprehended and sold by the overseers of the poor for any county or corporation in which he or she shall be found for the benefit of the poor of such county or corporation..." [11]

In 1816 the American Colonization Society was formed. This was a movement to return Africans to Africa. As more and more slaves were released from slavery, the push to return Africans to Africa became stronger. The two areas in Africa for repatriation were Liberia and Sierra Leone, both on the west coast of Africa.

In 1831, during the Nat Turner Insurrection, fifty-five white people were systematically slain by Nat Turner and other slaves in Southampton County, Virginia. Fear of insurrection for the white people of Northampton County was not was not a new emotion. In 1812, on the testimony of Edmund Francis and Nat (no last name given), Thomas Francis, John Francis, Edmund Press, Ben Wallace, and Babel Major were called to court to defend themselves against the charges of "making preparations for an insurrection." [12] In addition to the free Negroes called to court, there were several slaves: "Jonathan the property of Nathaniel Holland, Lewis the property of Edward Stratton and Sam & Jim the property of Laban Godwin." [13] In the end the charges were not founded and those involved were cleared of the charge of planning an insurrection.

As knowledge of the Nat Turner insurrection spread from locality to locality the fear of an uprising was recalled. White people began preparing themselves to prevent any hostile act. It was during this period in Virginia history that the bulk of the laws effecting free Negroes was passed. Legislation in 1831 was passed allowing localities to collect money for the express use of sending emancipated slaves to Liberia. During the period from 1831 to 1834 free Negroes lost all the gains made since the beginning of slavery.

During this period, the Eastern Shore of Virginia was one of the "main centers of hostility to free Negroes." Its isolation caused a greater sense of insecurity. It was this insecurity and possibly the memory of 1812 that led to the December 6, 1831 Petition to the Virginia Legislature. "Degraded by the stain which attaches to their color, excluded from many civil privileges which the humblest white man enjoys, and denied all participation in the government, it would be wholly absurd to expect from them any attachment to our laws and institution, or any sympathy with our people..." [14]

Shortly after this petition was received, the General Assembly approved the plan to raise not more than $15,000 for the removal of all free Negroes in Northampton County to Liberia. Between 1825 and 1840 Accomack and Northampton Counties met to discuss the problem of free Negroes. The result was that by 1840 several hundred free Negroes from Accomack had been driven out. But in Northampton the population of free Negroes decreased by almost half. In February 1832 a bill was passed allocating $35,000 in 1832 and $90,000 in 1833 for the express purpose of removing free Negroes to any place outside of the United States. [15]

These attempts at freeing the state of Virginia of emancipated Negroes failed. The fears and uncertainty of The Eastern Shore slave owners did not dissipate. Free Negroes and slaves were encouraged to inform on one another. Further legislation proved to be more effective. Another Act passed in 1831 made it unlawful to teach free Negroes to read and write and unlawful for free Negroes to learn to read and write. This law also made it illegal for free Negroes to preach, hold religious service or assemble for any reason. Free Negroes were no longer able to acquire slaves with the exception of husbands, wives and children. Chapter XXII, sections 1 through 14 was a most far reaching Act in that it reduced several acts into one. This Act diminished free Negroes' standing within the county. Once self-supporting people had become slaves "without masters."

Finally in 1843 a real blow to the free Negro was struck in the way of additional legislation. Free Negroes were prohibited from selling or offering for sale any agricultural products without having a written certificate from a respectable white citizen. This legislation was operative in Richmond and Accomack Counties and later adopted by most of the Counties in Virginia. Over the years many free Negroes had acquired land for farming and the Act of December, 1843 made it necessary for many of these free Negroes to sell their property. A more damaging result of this act is that many free Negroes sold themselves into slavery so that they could eat, be clothed and have shelter.

In 1850, still not pleased with the few free Negroes left in the state of Virginia as well as in Northampton County, a special poll tax was levied against every free Negro male between the ages of twenty-one and fifty-five. The revenue from the poll tax was to fund the removal of free Negroes to Liberia. Northampton County was one of the areas most concerned with the removal of free Negroes. By 1861 the Virginia General Assembly had passed an act setting the rules for voluntary enslavement of Free Negroes. [16]

While the state of Virginia was passing laws the localities were enforcing the laws and making some their own. In Northampton County Order Book 44 we read, "It being represented to the Court, that there are free negroes residing and habitually remaining in this County, who have come from other counties contrary to law, it is therefore ordered, that the Sheriff and each of his deputies, and each of the constables of this County do arrest all such free negroes as may be found therein, and commit them to the jail of this County, to be dealt with as the law directs."[17]

The county ordered the overseers of the poor to " use extraordinary vigilance in regard to the free negro population...." The Commissioner of the Revenue was ordered to "...use extraordinary diligence in as-certaining the free negroes in this County in violation of law....."[18]

The smallest pleasure experienced by a person of African ancestry was frowned upon "....the commonwealth of Virginia, in and for the body of the said County present, that the practice of owner of waggons and carts in hiring out them and their horses on the Sabbath day, to be employed in conveying the slaves and free negroes of the said County from one part thereof to a remote part of the same, is contrary to the spirit and intention of the laws of this Commonwealth in relation to the said slaves and free negroes, and to injure and deprive the owners of the said slaves of their services. And the jurors further present, that the habit of free negroes in riding in gigs and carriages on the Sabbath, from one part of the said County to another, and in and about the said County is a nuisance which ought to be abated; that it renders the slaves dissatisfied with their condition in life, and is injurious to good morals and good order. The jurors desire to call the attention of the people of the said County to said practices, and to request, that the Magistrates, Sheriffs and Constables, will, in as ample a manner as the laws may warrant, present said practices..."[19]

In 1857 the justices of Northampton County were summoned to appear to consider the advisability of appointing a special police for the county. After the appointment was made the special police were required to present to the Justice of the Peace ".....any and all persons who may be found unlawfully tampering with any slave or slaves, or suspected of so doing..."[20]

A further order from the Northampton County Courts restricted the hours free negroes could be in the public. The order was that "....no slaves shall be allowed to be at Eastville or other Public place or places in this county off of his owner or hirers premises later than 8 o'clock P. M. after the first day of October and before the first day of April, or later than 9 o'clock P. M. after the first day of April and before the first day of October, without the lawful permission in writing of the said owner or hirer: and that no free negro shall be allowed to be at any Public place in this County after the hours prescribed above in regard to slaves. And it is further ordered that the Special Police as well as all Sheriffs and Constables of this County are authorized and empowered to arrest all offenders against this order and have them dealt with according to law."[21]

Up to and during the Civil War the laws were aggressively enforced. In 1862 the following Northampton County order was recorded: "Ordered, that the Clerk of the court make out copies of the fines section of chapter 104 of the Code of Virginia, and that the Sheriff do post the same at the several stores and public places in this county, and it is further ordered that any merchant or ordinary keeper* in this county, who shall in future sell any intoxicating drink to any free negro, the Court will cause the license granted to such merchant or ordinary keeper to be revoked."[22]

The laws relative to free Negroes that were passed touched every segment of his/her life. Laws that were passed relative to African slaves also touched the lives of free Negroes. The registration of free Negroes was only one of many. As can be seen from the list contained in this book there was a fee for registration and a count for each period was kept in the register. For the specified fee an identification card (free papers) was issued to each registrant. The registrant was expected to carry the free papers on his or her person at all times in public. The case of Shadrack Bevans shows us that Northampton County officials were very serious about enforcing the law of registration for free negroes.

In November, 1837 the Grand Jury of Northampton returned "....the following presentment viz: We the Grand Jury do present Shadrack Bevans free negro, late of Accomack County for going at large & hiring himself out in the county without a certificate of register within the last month...Ordered, that Shadrack Bevans free negro, be summoned to appear here at the next quarterly Court, to shew cause, if any he can, why an information should not be filed against him upon a presentment of the Grand Jury this day made against him."[23]

A summons was issued against Shadrack Bevans and he was ordered to present himself to the Northampton County Court on the second of June, 1838. I would like to note that Shadrack Bevans is listed in the Register of Free Negroes as having registered between August 31, 1859 and August 31, 1860. Prior to this Shadrack Bevans was registered and certified in a court order in 1837.

"The Commonwealth of Virginia against Shadrack Bevans, Deft. Upon a Rule to Shew cause why an information should not be filed against him upon a presentment of the Grand Jury made against him. This day came the attorney for the Commonwealth & the defendant being solemnly called & not appearing: it is ordered that the said Rule be absolute & that an information be filed against the said Defendant upon the presentment aforesaid."[24] On June 13th, 1838 information was filed against Shadrack Bevans and he was ordered to appear at the next court quarterly session.

At the next session Shadrack Bevans appeared with his attorney, William I. Joynes, and stated that he was not guilty in "manner or form as in the said information against him is alleged & of this he putteth himself upon the county ..."[25] At the end of this proceeding Shadrack Bevans was found not guilty and was discharged from the court.

As we can see from a review of the registry of Shadrack Bevans, the act of registering did not always insure that there would not be confrontation with the authorities in Northampton County or for that matter in any locality in Virginia. Registration was the law for all free Negro people, wherever they lived.

When we compare *The Register of Free Negroes* to the United States Census for the period of 1850, many of the names in the Census do not appear for any year in the *Register of Free Negroes*. Many families that this writer knows from the Shore are absent. It is my belief that there wasn't the money for each free Negro in each household to be registered and so those that "needed" to be registered were registered. Those who found it necessary to go "at large" registered; those who could stay at home did not register.

Another reason for the absence of some names is that many free Negroes were forced out of Northampton County. Several members of the Francis Family were found in the records of Rochester, New York and several were found in Philadelphia, Pennsylvania. Several members of the Collins Family were found in the records of Philadelphia, Pennsylvania. There is the possibility that some free Negro citizens were sent to Liberia or Sierra Leone by the state of Virginia.

Attention is called to the instances where men in the register were described as having "holes in ears for rings". I believe that these men may have been a part of Gingaskin Indians. The Gingaskins Indians lived on the "seaside" of Eastville in Gingascount (Indian Town). This was a large tribe of Indians. It survived longer as a group than any other on the Eastern Shore of Virginia. Gingascount was also a place of refuge (called a maroon) for free Negroes and landless white people. The tribe was finally so racially mixed that they were essentially thought of as Negroes. Many lived in Gingascount until 1831, when the change in the social and political climate forced them to sell their land and many left Virginia. The last property sold by an owners was on May 16, 1860 by the Francis family. The Francis family which owned the last land in Indian Town lived in Rochester, New York and Philadelphia, Pennsylvania. Other surnames found in this book associated with the Gingaskin Indians are Collins, Carter, Bingham, Baker, Bevans (Bibbins), Drighouse (Driggus, Driggers), and House. The descendants of many of these people still live on the Eastern Shore of Virginia.

This Register of Free Negroes is being published in its original form and in its entirety. The spelling errors that appear in the original form are a part of this book; as are the punctuation, grammatical and capitalization errors. The wills which emancipated several of the Free Negro entries have been included as well as a guide to names that have been identified with African immigrants. Through the years spellings of some of these name changed. There are documented in this book the names of over five hundred free Negroes living between 1831 and 1861 in Northampton County. There are two hundred ninety-three free Negroes in the *Register of Free Negroes*, one hundred eighty-eight in the Certification of Free Negroes (Appendix I) and those slaves freed by wills in Appendix III, but who do not appear in the *Register of Free Negroes* itself. All of those listed here were born in Virginia. The names include African Americans freed by will, by deed and those whose families were freed during the seventeenth century.

We have included all of the relevant Virginia Laws from 1639 to 1861. These laws have been included to help establish the climate in which African immigrants, both free and slave, lived. These laws are also presented to document the official course Virginia took during its development. There were other laws passed which effected African immigrants, but to a lesser degree. The laws presented here are those that changed the course of every African immigrant both past and present.

In its published form this register is meant to be a tool for African Americans (1) studying the history of the African American immigrants and (2) researching family genealogy. For the public at large *The Register of Free Negroes* is a part of American History, a link to our common past. This is a part of the history of the Eastern Shore, Virginia and the United States.

FOOTNOTES

1. Ames, Susie M, *County Court Records, Northampton-Accomack, Virginia, 1640-1645*, page 32.
2. Ibid., pages 422-423.
3. Russell, John H., *The Free Negro*, 1619-1865.
4. Hening, ed., *Statutes at Large*, vol. 1, page 552.
5. Ibid., vol 1, page 145.
6. Grant, Joanne, ed., *Black Protest*, page 26.
7. Ibid., pages 26-27.
8. Mariner, Kirk, *Revival's Children*, page 95.
9. Weeks, *Southern Quakers and Slavery*, pages 212-214.
10. Hening, ed., *Statutes at Large*, vol. 2, pages 490-492.
11. Hening, ed., *Statutes at Large*, XVI, page 252.
12. Northampton County Order Book 35, pages 278-282
13. Ibid.
14. December 6, 1831, Petition from Northampton County to the General Assembly.
15. Virginia Act of Assembly, 1830-1831.
16. Virginia Act of Assembly, Chapter 75, Section 1-2.
17. Northampton County Order Book 44, page 227.
18. Ibid.
19. Northampton County Order Book 44, page 281.
20. Northampton County Order Book 44, page 425.
21. Ibid.
22. Northampton County Order Book 44, page 611.
23. Northampton County Order Book 40, page 75.
24. Northampton County Order Book 40, page 134
25. Northampton County Order Book 40, page 174.

* ordinary keeper was a person keeping an establishment in which spiritous beverages were served.

NOTES ON THE REGISTER OF FREE NEGROES

The Register of Free Negroes, located in the Northampton County Clerk's Office in Eastville, Virginia contains nine (9) separate entries:

NO- The first entry of the *Register of Free Negroes* assigns each registrant a number which is entered in numerical order.

AGE- The column for age sometimes provides us with just the year; a month and a year; a month, day and a year; or the age as of a specific date. There were many discrepancies in recording the ages. There are several entries without any date or age.

NAME- There are two hundred and ninety-three free Negro people registered. There are fifty-seven different surnames. In some instances people were registered more than once. It is believed that the free Negro population, in sympathy and out of concern for the African slave, very often gave their "free papers" to slaves to aid in their escape from the area.

COLOR- Each person is described first by color. The colors used are difficult to understand in light of descriptive adjectives used today. The colors include chesnut (dark or light), roan, light black, yellow, and mulatto (sometimes bright mulatto). The term mulatto is the only term that is descriptive of color in a technical sense. I would like to note that the word chestnut is spelled "chesnut" throughout the descriptions of the registered free Negroes. I have likewise used the spelling "chesnut."

STATURE- The third column refers to the physical size of each Negro. It is interesting to note how small each person was.

APPARENT MARKS OR SCARS ON FACE, HEAD OR HANDS- All marks or scars are recorded for each free Negro. Very often the very smallest imperfection is noted. In some cases words such as "sprightly" or "open countenance" were used to indicate a personality type of some of the individuals.

In the original manuscript there are three additional columns and headings. In this book those columns are included in the last column, Apparent Marks or Scars or Face, Head or Hands. Those additional columns include (1) By what instrument Emancipated, and when and where recorded. (2) In what County or place born free. Under this heading you will find the county in Virginia that the free Negro was born. There is also the entry "dd". It has been determined that this means <u>delivered</u>. The ones that simply show "dd" means that the free Negro took his /her "free papers" with him/her. If instead of "dd" another name appears it means that the free papers were sent to that person to give to the free Negro. These were sent to the second party for delivery. (3) If emancipated since May 1st, 1806, has permission been granted to live in what state, and by what Court and where. The Act of 1806 required free Negroes to move within twelve months after emancipation. There are no examples of permission granted to any free Negro to live in Northampton County.

In the original manuscript the will or deed is noted as the instrument of emancipation, but the wills and deeds are not provided. In an effort to make research easier, we have included each will and deed. In one instance (Mary Wilmer), the will was not recorded in the Northampton County Clerk's Office. Mary Wilmer, the daughter of Sylvia Wilmer, had been owned by Simon Wilmer. Mr. Wilmer originally lived in Northampton County, Virginia and served as a Rector for the Episcopal churches from 1819 to 1824. He was then sent to Charles County Maryland. There he served as the Rector of Christ Church and Chapel of the Saint John's Parish, Prince Georges and Charles Counties. His slaves were left in Virginia as were the slaves of his wife, Mary Eleanor Wilmer.

Northampton County records several things about this family: (1) Simon Wilmer was the owner of Sylvia Wilmer and her children. During the time he lived in Virginia (2) he was cited by the Court of Northampton for letting the children move around alone. As this was not the accepted behavior for a slave child.

After the death of Simon Wilmer, Sylvia was freed, but her children were held in slavery until they each reached the age of twenty-five. Mary applied twice for permission to live in the County of Northampton. All applications were denied. Mary appears as entry 49 in the Register of Free Negroes, having been registered between August 31, 1855 and August 31, 1856.

GUIDE TO AFRICAN-AMERICAN NAMES

On the Eastern Shore of Virginia there are several surnames that are associated with African-Americans. Please note that while these names may be thought of as African-American this does not mean that white Americans may not share these names.

Over the years these names may have changed in the spelling. In your reading these names may be spelled in several different ways. Record keepers during the 17th, 18th and 19th centuries very often wrote names as they thought they heard them. Very little time was taken in correctly spelling the names of African-Americans.

NAMES	ALTERNATE SPELLING
Ames	Aims
Belote	Beloat
Bibbins	Bevans, Beavans, Bevins, Bivins, Beavins, Beveans
Collins	Colins
Cotter	Carter
Cottrell	Cotral
Doughty	Dowty
Fitchett	Fitchette
Francis	Frances
Giddens	Giddings, Gittens
Harmon	Harman, Harmanson
Jubilee	Inbilee
Pool	Liverpool
Read	Reed, Reid
Simpkins	Simkins
Stevens	Stephens
Thompson	Tomson, Thomson, Thomason
Roselle	Rozelle, Rozell, Russel
Weeks	Weaks, Weicks, Wickes
Wescoat	Weskert, Wescot, Waiscoat

Additionally the names Drigus, Drighouse, Driggens, Driggers may all be derived from the name Rodriguez and may at some point in your reading refer to the same person or family.

The name Scisco (Sisco) may be a shortened version of Francisco. John and Arisbian Franscisco (Francisco) were among the first free Africans on the Eastern Shore of Virginia. It is possible that they were among the first African-American landowners.

The name Mingo is probably a short form of Domingo. Domingo, Francisco and Rodriguez are the names of several of the first Africans brought to the main land of Virginia in 1619. It is believed that the first Africans brought to Virginia came via the West Indies where they had been taken by the Spaniards.

Additionally, there are families living presently in Nigeria with surnames of Spanish origin. These people were taken as slaves from Nigeria to Brazil. After slavery was abolished in Brazil, they were able to return to Nigeria. They kept their Spanish names. These names of Spanish/Portuguese origin include Domingo, Parrera, DeSilva and DeCosta. I am sure that there are others that we have not documented.

In a book *Black Names in America: Origins and Usage*, Collected by Newbell Niles Puckett, it is stated that there exists, "a strong possibility that the majority of slaves brought into the Colonies before 1700 had Spanish names." To say the majority may seem to be a large percentage, but we are given to believe that many people brought into the Colonies as slaves had not come immediately from Africa.

The name Liverpool appears to have been shortened to Pool. There is evidence that there were Africans brought to Virginia by English ships trading out of Liverpool, England. Liverpool is said to have been one of the greatest slave trading port in the old world. Africans coming into Virginia on ships from Liverpool may have been called Liverpool to differentiate them from Africans from another ship or port.

The names that were given to Africans at birth were discarded when they arrived in the new world.. There are several instances where Africans steadfastly refused to give up their African names. I can find none of these examples in Africans that I have researched in Northampton County.

Number.	Age.	NAME.	Color.	Stature Ft. Inch.	Apparent Marks or Scars on Face, Head or Hands.
91	Born April 2nd A.D. 1818	Ned Moses	Dark Chesnut	5 8½	Scar on the right eye brow, also one in the middle of the forehead; Forehead receding; and inclined to baldness. Good countenance.
92	Born January 5th A.D. 1815	Smith Buckhouse	Yellow	5 9	Scar on the forehead, about one inch long — Flesh mole on right side of the nose — Several scars on the back of the right hand.
93	Born June 20th A.D. 1834	Jack Brickhouse	Black	5 10½	Scar on the back of the right hand near the little finger. Scar under the left ear of considerable size.
94	Born March 1st A.D. 1831	Michael Roan	Dark Mulatto	5 11	Large scar on the left hand including part of the wrist & thumb, caused by a burn. Fore finger on the left hand crooked. Thick lips.
95	Born March 15th A.D. 1838	John Becket	Mulatto	5 3½	Long scar on the left hand near the thumb — Scar on the forehead near the left eye brow — Black straight hair

By what instrument Emancipated, and when and where Recorded.	In what County or place born free.	If Emancipated since May 1st, 1806, w[hat] permission has been granted to reside [in] State, and by what Court and when.
	Northampton	
	(d.d)	
	Northampton	
	(d.d to h. J Scott)	
	Northampton	
	(d.d to h. J Scott)	
Last Will and testament of John Stockly Northampton County August 9th: 1847.		Permission has not been gra[nted] to Michael Roan to resid[e in] the State of Virginia, by [the] County Court of Northampt[on]
	(d.d)	
	Northampton	

No	Age	Name	Color	Stature ft inch	Apparent Marks or Scars on Face, Head or Hands
1	1825	Mary Rozell	Chestnut	5 2	Open countenance -prominent eyebrows Scar on the palm of the left hand. Born free in the County of Northampton State of Virginia copy dd
2	1827	Sabra Rozell	Yellow	5 3	Open expression, high cheek bones, front teeth defective-dark mark on the left cheek about half inch in length- Born free in the County of Northampton State of Virginia. copy dd
3	Aug 1831	Tobey Savage	Dark Chesnut	5 2	Long narrow face, and open expression-and several small scars on the back of the right hand. Scar on the head about an inch long- near the forehead. Born free in the County of Northampton State of Virginia. copy dd
4	Jan 10th 1833	Joseph Pool	Bright Mulatto	5 4 7/10	Round full face, straight black hair, and regular features. Circular scar small under right eye-Very small mole on cheek beneath left eye-and small mole on the back of the left hand. Born free in the County of Northampton State of Virginia.
5	June 4th 1832	Joseph Upshur	Black	5 5 1/2	Round full face-high cheek bones-even set of teeth sound. Scar on the back left hand on the knuckle of fore finger. Born free in the County of Northampton State of Virginia. copy dd

year ending Aug 31. 1853
From Sept. 1, 1853

No	Age	Name	Color	Stature ft inch	Apparent Marks or Scars on Face, Head or Hands
6	Nov 1831	Isaac Savage	Dark chesnut	5 7 6/10	Sharp narrow face, left eye defective, small mole or mark on left cheek bone small scar on right wrist Born free in the County of Northampton State of Virginia. (dd)
7	1832	Sarah Rozell	Light Chestnut	5 6 1/2	Broad flat face-small scar on the left cheek, & a white spot in right eye on lower part of the iris-and a scar on the knuckle of the right fore finger, next to the back of the hand Born free in the County of Northampton State of Virginia

No	Age	Name	Color	Stature ft inch	Apparent Marks or Scars on Face, Head or Hands
8	Apr 1832	Samuel Carter	Black	5 7 1/2	Prominent brow, low forehead high cheek bones, and a scar about three quarters inch long in the middle of the forehead-and several little scars on the back of right hand. Born free in the County of Northampton State of Virginia (dd)
9	Jan 1813	Mary Satchell	Dark Chesnut	5 5 1/5	No very notable scars except on the nose, & that feature is very much marked and scared from the effects of small pox. Born free in the County of Northampton State of Virginia (dd)
10	Oct 1838	Pricilla Anthony	Light Chesnut	5 3 9/1	Scar on right wrist and also one one the back of right hand-and small scar on the knuckle the third finger of the left hand. Born free in the County of Northampton State of Virginia (dd)
11	Mar 1833	Caleb Collins	Yellow	5 7 1/2	No very remarkable scars except a small one where the hair joins the forehead in a straight line from the left eye. Countenance open and expressive of good nature. Born free in the County of Northampton State of Virginia (dd)
12	Oct 16th 1833	Rosena Stephens	Bright Mulatto	5 0 1/2	Very small mole on the right cheek & also three very small moles on the chin-Regular handsome features-hair nearly straight Three small moles in palm of the left hand and two on the back of right hand. Born free in the County of Northampton State of Virginia (dd)
13	Mar 18th 1833	Polly Francis	Bright Mulatto	5 3 2/10	One of the butter or front teeth gone-small scar over or on the brow of the right eye small scar under left eye. Blue eyes-Features regular and face expressive of amiability, Scar on the third knuckle of the left hand. Born free in the County of Northampton State of Virginia
14	Mar 10th 1827	Johnson Brickhouse	Black	5 10	Scar on right cheek near the chin and on the jaw bone, high prominent forehead-& good expression of countenance. Born free in the County of Northampton State of Virginia.

No	Age	Name	Color	Stature ft inch	Apparent Marks or Scars on Face, Head or Hands
15	Mar 27th 1836	Louisa Upshur	Dark Chesnut	5 6 8/10	Round face, regular features, holes in ears for earrings-Scar aboat half an inch in length on the back knuckle of the fore finger of the left hand Born free in the County of Northampton State of Virginia. (dd)
16	Dec 1816	Amy Stephens	Black	5 1 1/5	Short, broad face-scar about half an inch long over left eyebrow-A small mole in the palm of each hand- Born free in the County of Northampton State of Virginia. (dd)
17	Jan 8th 1833	Jacob Collins	Yellow	5 6 3/10	Scar on left cheek, about an inch and a half in length-small mole on the forehead near the right eye brow and some small scars on the back of each hand. Born free in the County of Northampton State of Virginia (dd)
18	Apr 1833	William Edw. Harmon	Yellow	5 6	Scar in the middle of the fore head about three quarters of an inch long Sprightly face expressive of good humor-small scar on the left thumb just above the joint-two scars on the left leg-one on the bend near the knee and the other the shin. Born free in the County of Northampton State of Virginia. (dd)
19	Nov 1832	William Wallace	Yellow	5 7	Prominent features-small mole on the left side of neck-no notable scars on the on the face head or hands-Rather a serious expression of countenance- Born free in the County of Northampton State of Virginia. (dd)
20	Apr 18th 1815	Sabra Francis	Dark Chesnut	5 2	Pleasing countenance-full face-teeth defective-and some of the front ones gone-no notable scars Born free in the County of Northampton State of Virginia. (copy dd)
21	Nov 7th 1812	Abel Francis	Mulatto	5 7 3/10	Straight black hair-grey eyes-small scar on right cheek about an inch below the eye-small scars on the fore and middle fingers of right hand. Born free in the County of Northampton State of Virginia copy dd

No	Age	Name	Color	Stature ft inch	Apparent Marks or Scars on Face, Head or Hands
22	Sept 10th 1831	James Church	Dark Chesnut	5 8 3/10	Scar on the right arm near the elbow-Scar on wrist of right hand-high eye brows and face eye brows face rather narrow-nose thick and bulky. Born free in the County of Northampton State of Virginia copy dd
23	Jan 12th 1836	Adah Collins	Chesnut	5 1	Fore teeth separated-Small mole under the bottom lip, and some small scars on the left hand, and also some scars on the the left hand, and also some scars on the right hand. Born free in the County of Northampton State of Virginia. (dd)

Year - ending Aug 31st 1854=17 Registers
From Sept 1st 1854 -

No	Age	Name	Color	Stature ft inch	Apparent Marks or Scars on Face, Head or Hands
24	Feb 10th 1834	George Lecato	Very Dark Chesnut	5 7 1/5	Scar about half an inch long on right eyelid-Oblong face-Scar on the knuckle of the little finger of the left hand, and some small scars on the back of the left hand Born free in the County of Northampton State of Virginia. (dd)
25	Mar 1835	Jane Anthony	Mulatto	4 11 7/10	Round face-Regular Features scar on the forehead near the hair and in a straight line above the left eye, Scar on the right wrist about two inches in length. Born free in the County of Accomack State of Virginia. (dd)
26	Mar 16th 1832	John Morris	Yellow	5 3	A little crosseyed, hair of yellowish tinge; no remarkable scars on face, head or hands. Born free in the County of Northampton State of Virginia. (dd)
27	Mar 16th 1833	Michael Morris	Light Chesnut	5 10 1/2	Broad face, round forehead, and countenance expressive of good nature-small scars on the the right hand,-and a wart on the little finger of the left hand. Born free in the County of Northampton State of Virginia. (dd)
28	Feb 11th 1832	Elizabeth Church	Light Chesnut	5 2 3/10	Open good expresion of countenance; small scar about an inch long on the left cheek, some small scars on the back of the right hand; and a mole on the neck. Born free in the County of Northampton State of Virginia (dd)

No	Age	Name	Color	Stature ft inch	Apparent Marks or Scars on Face, Head or Hands
29	Jan 11th 1837	Mary Ann Satchell	Light Chesnut	5 2	High cheek bones, round forehead, and a scar forming a semicircle on the upper part of the forehead. Born free in the County of Northampton State of Virginia (dd)
30	Sept 8th 1834	Horace Francis	Light Chesnut	5 8	Small features,-blue eyes-small scar below the right eye-dimple in the chin-good expression of countenance. Born free in the County of Northampton State of Virginia (dd)
31	Aug 22nd 1833	John Stephens	Yellow	5 7	Scar about three-quarters of an inch long between the eye brows, regular features; and two small moles on the back of right hand. Born free in the County of Northampton State of Virginia (dd)
32	Mar 1830	Joseph Stephens	Yellow	5 6 1/2	Scar about an inch long near the corner of the left eye; mole on the right side of the neck just below the jaw bone; good expression of countenance. Born free in the County of Northampton State of Virginia (dd)
33	1833	Nathaniel Sutton	Black	4 7 1/2	Broad face, flat nose, good forehead, thick lips, scar on the forehead just above the right eyebrow. Born free in the County of Northampton State of Virginia (dd)
34	1823	Margaret Gleeson	Mulatto	5 1 1/2	Scar on the right side of the neck-hair straight-small mole on the right cheek near the neck; grey eyes, and amiable expression of countenance; small scar on palm of left hand; and on forefinger of left hand. Born free in the County of Northampton State of Virginia (dd)
35	Jan 2nd 1826	Peter Satchell	Black	5 6 7/10	Scar in the middle of the forehead, lips thick; two of the upper front teeth out, and some of the others defective; and a mole on the forefinger of the right hand. Born free in the County of Northampton State of Virginia (dd)
36	Apr 4th 1802	Henry Morris	Chesnut	6 0 1/5	Small scar on the forehead over the right eye brow, short broad nose, large eyes, and features generally prominent-some small scars on the back of each hand. Born free in the County of Northampton State of Virginia (dd)

No	Age	Name	Color	Stature ft inch	Apparent Marks or Scars on Face, Head or Hands
37	July 4th 1836	Smith Satchell	Light Chesnut	5 7 1/4	Oblong face, small scar near the right temple, small scar in the forehead, a scratch on the left cheek, and large scar on the back of the right hand & scar on the thumb of the left hand.
					Born free in the County of Northampton State of Virginia (dd)
38	Feb 16th 1834	Robert Satchell	Mulatto	5 2 1/2	Scar on the head about two inches long-Small scars scars on the back of each hand-holes in the ears for rings-hair straight-grey eyes.
					Born free in the County of Northampton State of Virginia (dd)
39	Aug 15th 1833	Elizabeth Christian	Dark Chesnut	4 11 3/4	Regular features, pleasant expression of countenance; some scars on the knuckles of the right hand and scar about an inch long on the back of the left hand.
					Born in the County of Northampton State of Virginia
40	Sept 1834	George Read	Yellow	5 9 1/2	Some small scars on the forehead, also on the back of the neck; and also some small scars on the back of of each hand.
					Born in the County of Northampton State of Virginia (dd)
41	Jun 1834	Horace Read	Chesnut	5 6	Scar on the forehead about one half of an inch long- and some scars on thumb of the left hand.
					Born in the County of Northampton State of Virginia (dd)
42	Mar 1827	Jim Spady	Light Chesnut	5 9	High cheek bones, small mole on the right side of the nose-scar about an inch long on the back of right hand, and scar on the ball of the middle finger of left hand.
					Born in the County of Northampton State of Virginia (dd)
43	Aug 1834	Lucy Church	Chesnut	5 3 3/10	Broad face, and good expression, small scar on the left cheek-scar near the wrist on the back of left hand, & a scar on the fore finger of the left hand.
					Born in the County of Northampton State of Virginia (dd)
44	Aug 20th 1833	George Stephens	Chesnut	5 3	Scar under left eye; one of front teeth out; Scar on right wrist about three inches long- Scar on fore finger
					Born in the County of Northampton State of Virginia (dd)

Year ending Aug 31st = 1855 = 22 Registers:

No	Age	Name	Color	Stature ft inch	Apparent Marks or Scars on Face, Head or Hands
45	Dec 15th 1831	Rachel Poulson	Chesnut	5 4	Small scar on the nose-good expression- scar on left hand near the wrist Scar on the back of the right hand near the wrist.
					Born in the County of Northampton State of Virginia (dd)
46	Oct 21st 1834	William Carter	Black	5 8	Scar on the fore head above the right eye; Scar on the inside of the left wrist-and some small scars on the back of each hand.
					Born in the County of Northampton State of Virginia (dd)
47	1812	Ann Satchell	Mulatto	5 0	Small scar on left cheek; Small scar back of left hand, and also a mole on left hand near the wrist. Walks lame.
					Born in the County of Northampton State of Virginia (dd)
48	Mar 1835	John Satchell	Chesnut	5 9	Holes in the ears for rings-some small scars and scratches on the back of the right hand.
					Born in the County of Northampton State of Virginia (dd)
49	Jan 1830	Mary Wilmer	Light Chesnut	5 0	Small scar near the right corner of the mouth-and some moles on the left side of the neck; & small scar on the right wrist-& some notable scars on each arm.
					Emancipated by the will of Simon Wilmer, decd., proved July 14th A. D. 1840, in the Orphan's Court for Charles County, in the State of Maryland-as appears by a certified copy thereof filed in the Clerk's Office of Northampton, County Court.
					Permission has not been granted to Mary Wilmer to reside in the State of Virginia, by the County Court of Northampton County. (dd)
					Note:-Mary is one of the children of Sylvia, liberated at the age of twenty five years by Simon Wilmer's Will.
					Copy of will emancipating Mary Wilmer not found in Northampton Clerk's Office.
50	Oct 20th 1828	Henry Morris Jr	Dark Chesnut	5 11 4/10	Two moles on the left side of the face, one near the eye, the other near the mouth; Small scar on the right forefinger on the right hand; Small scar on the back of the left hand near the forefinger
					Born free in the County of Northampton State of Virginia (dd)

No	Age	Name	Color	Stature ft inch	Apparent Marks or Scars on Face, Head or Hands
51	Mar 15th 1834	Esther Collins	Mulatto	5 2	Regular features and good expression of countenance; and some very small moles under the eyes and on the nose. Born free in the County of Northampton State of Virginia. sent by Ro. C. Jacob
52	About 1790	Littleton Church	Dark Chesnut	5 7	Scar on the inside of right wrist; scar on the forehead in a distinct line above the left eye Born free in the County of Northampton State of Virginia. sent by Ro. C. Jacob.
53	1833	Mary Stephens	Yellow	5 2 1/2	Scar on the left hand just above the knuckles of the forefinger -face freckled very much below the eyebrows and above the mouth. Born free in the County of Northampton, State of Virginia. (dd)
54	Jan 1st 1835	Mahala Ames	Yellow	5 0 1/2	Scar on the thumb of the left hand-thick lips-features regular- forehead good- Born free in the County of Northampton State of Virginia copy sent Deward Fitchett
55	Aug 8th 1832	Margaret Collins	Mulatto	5 1 1/2	Some small scars on the left cheek; scar on the thumb;scar on the forefinger and several other small scars on the left hand; nail on second finger of right hand injured. Born free in the County of Northampton, State of Virginia. copy sent Ro. C. Jacob Esq.
56	Mar 2nd 1842	Joseph Bevans	Black	4 11 1/5	Some small scars on the back of the right hand; hand; small features-forehead narrow and nose not very flat. Born free in the County of Northampton State of Virginia sent by Deward Fitchett
57	May 11th 1829	Elizabeth Bevans	Black	5 2 4/5	Scar on left cheek;front teeth separated; and small mole on the right nostril, & one also on the upper lip. Born free in the County of Northampton State of Virginia. sent by D. Fitchett
58	Sept 1st 1827	Elizabeth Johnson	Black	5 2 4/5	Large scar on the out side of left wrist about one inch long with a protuberance on the middle; little finger on the left hand crooked; Scar on inside of right wrist about 1/2 inch long Born free in the County of Northampton, State of Virginia. sent by Dew: Fitchett

No	Age	Name	Color	Stature ft inch	Apparent Marks or Scars on Face, Head or Hands
59	Aug 10th 1795	Esther Bevans	Dark Chesnut	5 3 1/2	Mole behind right ear. Two natural marks on leftcheek. Mole under left side of nose. Mole on middle finger on right hand.
					Born free in the County of Northampton State of Virginia. sent by Dew: Fitchett
60	Dec 5th	Henry Collins	Yellow	5 3 1/10	Small scar on right cheek, Scar on left thumb.
					Born free in the County of Northampton State of Virginia. sent by Ro. C. Jacob
61	Dec 1823	Esther Perkins	Dark Chesnut	5 1 1/2	Large scar over right eye-Small scar in middle of forehead-small scar on fore finger on left hand-Little finger crooked on right hand
					Born free in the County of Northampton State of Virginia. sent by Jacob Nottingham
62	Jan 1833	James Webb	Black	5 4 1/5	Small scar under the left middle finger on the left hand crooked.
					Born free in the County of Northampton State of Virginia. (dd sent by Jacob Nottingham)
63	Aug 1832	Emily Brickhouse	Dark Chesnut	5 6/10	Flat nose-Mole on left temple-Scar on right wrist-Three scars on right thumb.
					Born free in the County of Northampton State of Virginia. (dd)
64	Feb 8th 1802	Sally Giddens	Nearly Black	5 3 1/2	Small Scar from a burn on the right hand, near the thumb, and one on the thumb.
					Born free in the County of Accomack State of Virginia. (dd to son) Wm.
65	Aug 1819	Rachel Brickhouse	Dark Chesnut	5 2 7/10	Small mole between the chin and lower lip, burnt mark on middle and ring finger-Mole on middle finger of left hand near the nail
					Born free in the County of Northampton State of Virginia. (dd)
66	Aug 1833	Drucilla Brickhouse	Light Chesnut	5 1/10	Small scar on the under lip. Mole on the under lip. Face tolerably broad.
					Born free in the County of Northampton State of Virginia. (dd)

No	Age	Name	Color	Stature ft inch	Apparent Marks or Scars on Face, Head or Hands
67	1809	Sophia Griffin	Dark Yellow	5 1	Mole on left cheek near the nose, few small pox marks on the nose-Long scar on the middle finger Mole on the left hand near the wrist
					Born free in the County of Accomack State of Virginia. sent by Ro. C. Jacob
68	1805	Levi Matthews	Black	5 11 1/10	Scar on left cheek bone, near the eye; Scar on the cheek near the nose.
					Born free in the County of Northampton State of Virginia (dd)
69	Mar 9th 1830	Bridget Brickhouse	Dark Chesnut	5 1/10	Mole under lip; Mole on left cheek near the nose, One checken pox scar on left cheek; Scar on left thumb.
					Born free in the County of Northampton State of Virginia (dd)
70	Dec 1832	Caroline Brickhouse	Light Chesnut	5 4/10	Scar on fore finger on right hand. Scar on middle finger on right hand. Scar on right wrist.
					Born free in the County of Northampton State of Virginia (dd)
71	Jan 1824	Arthur Stephens	Yellow	5 3 1/2	Small mole on left cheek bone; Freckled; Scar on middle finger on right hand.Scar over the first bone of the thumb on left hand.
					Born free in the County of Northampton State of Virginia (dd)
72	Sept 8th 1834	Michael Johnson	Yellow	6 4/10	Small scar in the middle of forehead small mole on the right cheek-face bompy-Small scar on back of the left hand.
					Born free in the County of Northampton State of Virginia (dd to T. W. Jacob)
73	May 5th 1832	James Giddens	Black	5 7 7/10	Scar on left cheek bone, Scar on left thumb; Scar on back of right hand.
					Born free in the County of Northampton State of Virginia (dd to T. W. Jacob)
74	July 1837	John Stevens	Black	5 6 3/10	Small scar in the middle of the forehead. Narrow face. Scar on back of the right hand. Scar on back of the left hand near the thumb. & one near the little finger on left hand.
					Born free in the County of Northampton State of Virginia (dd)

No	Age	Name	Color	Stature ft inch	Apparent Marks or Scars on Face, Head or Hands
75	Dec 1830	Mary Ann Brickhouse	Dark Brown	5 1 7/10	Scar on left cheek bone; Scar on back of left hand near the thumb. Born free in the County of Northampton State of Virginia (dd)
76	No Date	Elizabeth Weeks	Dark Chesnut	5 7/10	Scar on the left hand near the thumb. Mole on the left hand near the thumb- Scar on the back of the left hand near the little finger. Scar on right hand near the wrist. Born free in the County of Northampton State of Virginia (dd)
77	Nov 1830	Susan Weeks	Black	5 3 6/10	Mole between the eyes. Small scar from a burn on the back of the right hand. Two moles in palm of left hand. Born free in the County of Northampton State of Virginia (dd)
78	Jan 1834	William Brickhouse	Yellow	5 8	Scar under the right eye-Scar on the cheek-MOle under left eye-Bushy head of hair. Scar on left little finger. Born free in the County of Northampton State of Virginia (dd)
79	Jan 1840	Elizabeth Brickhouse	Dark Brown	4 10 6/10	Scar from a burn between the lower lip & chin-Small scar on knuckle of right hand. Born free in the County of Northampton State of Virginia (dd)
80	Dec 25th 1828	George Stephens	Black	5 7	Scar on the right cheek near the mouth holes in the ears for rings,-that in the right ear torn out-& two small scars on the left eye brow- Born free in the County of Northampton State of Virginia (dd) W.I.F.P.
81	Dec 1828	Ann Collins	Light Brown	5 5 6/10	Mole on the left cheek,-Open countenance Born free in the County of Northampton State of Virginia (dd)
82	Jun 1st 1834	Mary Jane Collins	Chesnut	5 1 1/2	Scar from a cut on the right eye brow-holes 1st in the ears for rings. small scar on the back of right hand, and large mole on the right arm. Born free in the County of Northampton State of Virginia (dd)

No	Age	Name	Color	Stature ft inch	Apparent Marks or Scars on Face, Head or Hands
83	Sept 1834	Tamar Simkins	Light Chesnut	5 4 7/10	Scar on the middle of the right hand on the first joint. Scar on the back of the right hand. Scar on the left hand near the thumb. Scar on the left cheek. Born free in the County of Northampton State of Virginia. (dd)
84	July 1st 1834	James E. Collins	Light Yellow	5 11	Scar on the middle finger, on the left hand near the second joint. Scar on the thumb of the right hand, and on the fore finger of the right hand. Mole on the chin. Born free in the County of Northampton State of Virginia. (dd)
85	Oct 1st 1834	John Webb	Light Chesnut	5 7 7/10	Little of the left hand quite crooked. Scar on the end of the forefinger on the right hand. Small scar on the left cheek near the mouth. Born free in the County of Northampton State of Virginia. (dd) T.K.D.
86	Oct 25th 1834	Abel Church Jr	Light Brown	5 4 1/2	Small scar just under the nose, and One on left cheek bone. Born free in the County of Northampton State of Virginia. (dd)
87	Apr 27th 1837	Elizabeth S. Collins	Light Yellow	5 2 7/10	Scar on the left thumb Wine flesh mark on the left hand running up the arm some distance. Small scar on the left temple. Born free in the County of Northampton State of Virginia.
88	Mar 15th 1831	Adah N. Collins	Light Yellow	5 3 8/10	Little finger on the right hand crooked; Scar on the face near the left eye, and one on the left cheek bone. Born free in the County of Northampton State of Virginia. (dd)
89	Sept 20th 1834	Michael Only	Chesnut	5 6 4/10	Small scar on the left hand near the fore finger-Small scar on the left cheek bone- Born free in the County of Northampton State of Virginia. (dd to L. S. Read)

No	Age	Name	Color	Stature ft inch	Apparent Marks or Scars on Face, Head or Hands
90	Apr 13th 1831	Henry Pool	Yellow	5 8 1/10	Scar on the face near the left ear. Open countenance.
					Born free in the County of Northampton State of Virginia. (dd to T. W. J.)
91	Apr 2nd 1818	Ned Moses	Dark Chesnut	5 8 1/2	Scar on the right eye brow, also one in the middle of the forehead; Forehead receding; and inclined to balding; Good countenance-
					Born free in the County of Northampton State of Virginia. (dd)
92	Jan 5th 1815	Smith Brickhouse	Yellow	5 9	Scar on the forehead, abot one inch long- Flesh mole on right side of the nose- Several scars on the back of the right hand.
					Born free in the County of Northampton State of Virginia. dd to Jno. T. Scott
93	Jun 20th 1834	Jack Brickhouse	Black	5 10 1/5	Scar on the back of the right hand, near the little finger. Scar under the left ear of considerable size.
					Born free in the County of Northampton State of Virginia. dd to Jno. T. Scott
94	Mar 1st 1831	Michael Roan	Dark Mulatto	5 11	Large scar on the left hand, including part of the wrist & thumb, caused by a burn. Fore finger on the left hand crooked. Thick lips.
					Emancipated by Last will and testament of John Stockly. Northampton County August 9th 1847.
					Permission has not been granted to Michael Roan to reside in the State of Virginia, by the County of Northampton.
95	Mar 15th 1838	John Becket	Mulatto	5 3 1/2	Long scar on the left hand near the thumb- Scar on the forehead near the left eye brow- Black straight hair
					Born in the County of Northampton State of Virginia. (dd)
96	July 3rd 1834	Smith Collins	Chesnut	5 9	Scar on the left cheek just below the ear, holes in the ears for ear-rings, large scar on the inner side of the right wrist; and some scars on the back of right wrist and right hand.
					Born in the County of Northampton State of Virginia (dd)

No	Age	Name	Color	Stature ft inch	Apparent Marks or Scars on Face, Head or Hands
	.75 Tax on Seal ends here 1.50 Tax on Seal commences				
97	Aug 1835	Matilda Becket	Chesnut	5 1 1/2	Scar on the neck near the right cheek small moles on the forehead, between the eyebrows; holes in ears for rings-two small moles on back of left hand, and some small scars on the fingers of the left hand. Born in the County of Accomack State of Virginia. (dd)
	For year ending Aug: 31, 1856 = 53 Registers 52 @ .75 = 39.00 1 @ 1.50 = 1.50 } = $40.50				
98	Aug 30 1832	Nathan Drighouse	Dark Chesnut	5 8 6/10	Small scar over the right eye brow; very small mole on forehead, and also one on the nose. Scar on the little finger of left hand. Born in the County of Northampton State of Virginia. (dd)
99	Oct 15th 1831	John Johnson	Light Chesnut	5 3 7/10	Scar on the neck about one inch long, near jaw; Scar on the left hand, about one inch long on the second knuckle of the thumb. Small scar on the right hand-on the knuckle on the middle finger. Born in the County of Northampton State of Virginia. (dd)
100	Jun 27th 1833	John Satchell	Dark Chesnut	5 10 3/4	A scar on the fore head about half inch long and between the eyebrows; oblong face-Fore finger bent from a cut on the knuckle of the same on the left hand. Born in the County of Northampton State of Virginia. (dd)
101	About 1822	Lewis Fisher	Black	5 3 4/5	Small Scar near the right eye, and also a small scar on the left hand. Emancipated by The last will and testament of Arthur R. Savage, deceased-Recorded in the Clerk's Office of Northampton County Court on 13th Day of February A. D. 1837. Permission has not been granted to reside in this State-to the date January 12th 1857-by the Court of Northampton.
102	About 1820	David Heath	Dark Chesnut	5 10 1/5	Small scar on the right cheek, and also a scar about an inch long on the top of the head. Emancipated by The last will and testament of Arthur R. Savage, deceased-Recorded in the Clerk's Office of Northampton County Court on 13th Day of February A. D. 1837. Permission has not been granted to reside in this State-to the date January 12th 1857-by the Court of Northampton.

No	Age	Name	Color	Stature ft inch	Apparent Marks or Scars on Face, Head or Hands
103	Jan 15th 1834	Ralph Collins	Dark Chesnut	5 8 1/5	Mole on the right cheek. Good expression of countenance. Small scars on the back of each hand
					Born in the County of Northampton State of Virginia (dd)
104	Dec 26th 1835	James Collins	Black	5 9 1/5	Small scar on the right cheek, Round face, and expression of good nature. Scar and a mole on the back of the left hand.
					Born in the County of Northampton State of Virginia (dd)
105	Mar 20th 1836	Wesley Stephens	Black	5 7	Small scar under the right eye; Some small scars on the thumb of the left hand; oblong Oblong face, and good natured expression of countenance
					Born in the County of Northampton State of Virginia (dd) Tax and fee not paid

year ending Aug. 31, 1857: 8 Register

No	Age	Name	Color	Stature ft inch	Apparent Marks or Scars on Face, Head or Hands
106	Mar 1st 1834	Lewis Rozell	Chesnut	5 9 1/5	Small mole on the right cheek-very small scar on the forehead-and a scar on the forefinger of the left hand near the middle joint on knuckle.
					Born in the County of Northampton State of Virginia
107	Jun 1837	William Lecato	Black	5 0 1/2	Sink or hole on the top of the head, from the kick of a horse-round face, and amiable expression of countenance
					Born in the County of Northampton State of Virginia (dd)
108	Jan 8th 1830	Ann Eliza Collins	Mulatto	5 4 4/10	Small scar on each eyebrow, very small mole on each cheek.
					Born in the County of Northampton State of Virginia (dd)
109	Jan 1835	Alfred Collins	Dark Chesnut	6 0 1/2	Scar near the left eye; two small scars near the right eye; holes in ears for rings, scar on the back of the right hand.
					Born in the County of Northampton State of Virginia (dd)

No	Age	Name	Color	Stature ft inch	Apparent Marks or Scars on Face, Head or Hands
110	Oct 1836	Levin Johnson	Black	5 5 1/2	Scar on the forehead-on the upper part near the hair-forehead narrow-countenance open, and expressive of good humor-Scar the right hand near the thumb. Born in the County of Northampton State of Virginia (dd)
111	Jun 4th 1832	Joseph Upshur	Black	5 5 1/2	Round full face-even and sound set of teeth-good expression of countenance-dimples on cheeks when laughing-and a scar on the knuckle of the forefinger of the left hand. Born in the County of Northampton State of Virginia (dd)

For year ending Aug: 31. 1858. six Registers @ 1.50_ $9.00

No	Age	Name	Color	Stature ft inch	Apparent Marks or Scars on Face, Head or Hands
112	May 20th 1804	Susy Jubilee	Dark Chesnut	5 6 1/2	Long face, prominent cheek bones most of the upper front teeth gone-two small moles on the little finger of the right hand. Born in the County of Northampton State of Virginia (dd)
113	May 27th 1832	Tabitha Brickhouse	Dark Chesnut	4 11 1/2	Oblong face, round forehead-and very small mole on the middle finger of the left hand; and a small mole on the chin. Born in the County of Northampton State of Virginia (dd)
114	Sept 13th 1837	William Pitts	Black	5 7 8/10	Oblong face-no apparent marks or scars except holes in ears for ring Born in the County of Northampton State of Virginia (dd)
115	Apr 15th 1837	Henry Collins	Mulatto	5 10	Some small scars on each hand; small mole on the on the left cheek and a small mole also on the nose-and straight black hair. Born in the County of Northampton State of Virginia (dd)
116	Feb 14th 1841	Nancy Pool	Chesnut	5 2	Mole on the thumb of the left hand, and two small moles on the left hand, and a small mole on the left cheek. Born in the County of Northampton State of Virginia (dd)

No	Age	Name	Color	Stature ft inch	Apparent Marks or Scars on Face, Head or Hands
117	Jun 5th 1845	Betsy Poulson	Chesnut	5 0 1/2	Small scar on the right wrist, near the hand; small mole on the nose near the corner of the eye.
					Born in the County of Northampton State of Virginia (dd)
118	Aug 1838	Wesley Brickhouse	Dark Chestnut	5 6	Scar on the upper lip just below the left nostril; a scar on the inside of the left wrist.
					Born in the County of Northampton State of Virginia (dd)
119	Jan 29th 1837	Littleton Church	Dark Chesnut	5 6 1/2	Scar on the right cheek; scar on top of the head, and scar on the left hand near the wrist
					Born in the County of Northampton State of Virginia (dd)
120	Jan 1839	Jacob Lecato	Black	5 6 1\2	Scar on the bottom lip, small mole on the left cheek, and a scar from a burn on the back of the right hand.
					Born in the County of Northampton State of Virginia (dd)
121	Sept 20th 1857	Henry Giddens	Chesnut	5 6 1/2	Scar on the upper part of the thumb of the left hand; small mole on the left cheek, a small mole on the right cheek, and also a mole on the nose
					Born in the County of Northampton State of Virginia (dd)
122	Jan 4th 1832	Jane Lecato	Chesnut	5 1 1/2	Mole in the palm of the right hand, mole on the inside of the thumb of right hand, and a mole near the wrist of the left hand.
					Born in the County of Northampton State of Virginia (dd)
123	Mar 15th 1837	George Lecato	Chesnut	5 6 1/4	Scar on the upper lip; holes in the ears for rings; and a scar on the ____ of the forefinger of the right hand.
					Born in the County of Northampton State of Virginia (dd)
124	Oct 1828	Geraldine Savage	Chesnut	4 11	Scar near the corner of the right eye Scar on the upper lip: and a small under the left eye
					Born in the County of Northampton State of Virginia (dd)

No	Age	Name	Color	Stature ft inch	Apparent Marks or Scars on Face, Head or Hands
125	Oct 1831	John Aims	Yellow	5 5	Scar on the fore finger of the left hand.
					Born in the County of Northampton State of Virginia (dd)
126	Sept 2nd 1837	Chapman Stephens	Chesnut	5 7 1/10	Scar on the joint of the middle finger of the left hand.
					Born in the County of Northampton State of Virginia (dd)
127	July 12th 1838	Charles Pool	Chesnut	5 7 3/10	Small scar on the forehead and also one on the nose; and a scar about two inches long on the left arm.
					Born in the County of Northampton State of Virginia (dd)

16 Register Yr. end'g: Aug. 31, 1859 - @ 1 1/2 = $24.00

No	Age	Name	Color	Stature ft inch	Apparent Marks or Scars on Face, Head or Hands
128	May 2nd 1837	Emily Rozell	Light Chesnut	5 3 1/2	Mole on the middle finger of the left hand. Scar on the inside of the left hand near the thumb.
					Born in the County of Northampton State of Virginia (dd)
129	Nov 1st 1831	John Reid	Chesnut	5 6 1/2	Small scar in the middle of the forehead, some very small pox marks on the nose; and a scar on the end of the middle finger of the left hand.
					Born in the County of Northampton State of Virginia (dd)
130	No Date Given	Smith Morris	Yellow	5 9	Little crossed, small scar on the left cheek; a small mole on the forehead near his left temple; hair has a yellowish hue; and some small scars on the back of the right hand.
					Born in the County of Northampton State of Virginia (dd)
131	Jan 10th 1833	Joseph Pool	Mulatto	5 6	Small mole on the left cheek-small mole on the forehead-mole on the back of the left hand mole on the left thumb and a small mole between the fore and middle finger of the right hand.
					Born in the County of Northampton State of Virginia (dd)

No	Age	Name	Color	Stature ft inch	Apparent Marks or Scars on Face, Head or Hands
132	May 11th 1835	Peggy Brickhouse	Chesnut	5 3	Small mole on the left cheek about an inch below the eye; small scars on the back of the right hand- Scar on the wrist of the left hand caused by a burn.
					Born in the County of Northampton State of Virginia (dd)
133	Dec 23rd 1797	Shadrack Bevans	Yellow	5 5 1/2	Scar just below the under lip, and a scar on the back of the right hand, near the knuckle of the fore finger.
					Born in the County of Accomack State of Virginia (dd)
134	20yrs Dec 24th	Peggy Cottrel	Chesnut	5 1/2	Large Scar on the left side of the neck; Scar on the back of the right hand, between the thumb and fore finger
					Born in the County of Northampton State of Virginia (dd)
135	22yrs Sept 19th 1859	Wm. Henry Sisco	Chesnut	5 4 2/10	Long scar under the right eye; and a small mole under the same eye
					Born in the County of Northampton State of Virginia (dd)
136	13yrs Aug 7th 1859	Mary Ann Collins	Light Yellow	5 3 4/10	Dark place on the back of right hand from from a burn; round face and regular features
					Born in the County of Northampton State of Virginia (dd)
137	25yrs 1859	Emma Collins	Dark Chesnut	5 1 2/10	Holes in ears for rings small scar on the right cheek, and a small scar on the fore finger of the right hand.
					Born in the County of Northampton State of Virginia (dd)
138	31yrs in 1859	Noah Collins	Chesnut	5 6 4/10	A scar on the back of the left hand.
					Born in the County of Northampton State of Virginia (dd)
139	22yrs 11th Apr 1860	John Howell	Yellow	5 11 2/10	Face full of small moles-front teeth separated by a vacant space.
					Born in the County of Northampton State of Virginia (dd)

No	Age	Name	Color	Stature ft inch	Apparent Marks or Scars on Face, Head or Hands
140	21yrs 3rd Aug 1859	Agnes Satchell	Dark Yellow	5 3/10	One small mole on the right of the face near the nose-one on left D. Small scar on the palm of the left near the fore finger. Born in the County of Northampton State of Virginia (dd)
141	17yrs Sept 17th 1859	Peggy Satchell	Yellow	5 5 9/10	One scar on the right hand at the root of a the forefinger-one small on the right arm near the wrist- One small mole on the back of the neck. Born in the County of Northampton State of Virginia (dd)
142	39yrs 1st Jan 1859	Emeline Bevans	Light Chesnut	5 4	Small mole on left eyebrow, and several small moles on right cheek. Born in the County of Northampton State of Virginia (dd)
143	49yrs 1st Jan 1859	Robert Bevans	Dark Chesnut	5 4	Scar on left eye brow scar on thumb of the left hand. Born in the County of Northampton State of Virginia (dd)
144	25yrs 1859	Ann Reed	Yellow	5 5 2/10	Scar on the back of left hand, front separated by a small space- Born in the County of Northampton State of Virginia (dd)
145	Aug 2nd 1821	Rachel Stevens	Light Black	4 11	Scar about 3/4 inch long on left cheek, amll scar on throat immediately in front-large round mark (lighter than natural color) on inside left arm half way from wrist to elbow. Born in the County of Northampton State of Virginia (dd)
146	About 26 years old	Margaret Stephens	Chesnut	5 9/10	Scar on the left side of the face near the nose; Scar on the right cheek near the eye. Born in the County of Northampton State of Virginia (dd)

No	Age	Name	Color	Stature ft inch	Apparent Marks or Scars on Face, Head or Hands
147	19yrs 7th Sept 1859	Lavinia Collins	Light Chesnut	5 6 3/10	A small scar on the left cheek bone. A very small scar on the cheek, Scar in the middle of the forehead-Little finger on the right hand crooked slightly. Born in the County of Northampton State of Virginia (dd)
148	Dec 1820	Maria A. Collins	Dark Chesnut	5 6 7/10	Small scar near the right eye, near the mole of the head. Scar on the back of the right hand. Enlargement on the back of the right hand near the wrist. Born in the County of Northampton State of Virginia (dd)
149	41yrs 15th Dec 1859	Frederick Moses	Light Chesnut	5 10 1/2	One scar on right cheek; one scar on brow just above left eye, 3 scars on back of left hand-Cross-eyes. Born in the County of Northampton State of Virginia (dd)
150	25yrs 10th 1859	Esther Moses	Very Light Chesnut	5 1 3/10	2 scars on right wrist-2 scars on wrist-mark on left cheek (lighter than natural Born in the County of Northampton State of Virginia (dd)
151	26yrs 8th Jan 1859	Jacob Collins	Yellow	5 6 7/10	Scar on left cheek and holes in ears for rings, one scar on left thumb, several small scars on back of left hand. Born in the County of Northampton State of Virginia (dd)
152	Apr 1821	Vianna Collins	Light Black	5 6 7/10	Scar in the forehead-Scar over the left eye - Small scar on the back of the left hand Born in the County of Northampton State of Virginia (dd)
153	Dec 4th 1821	Jeptha Cottrell	Dark Chesnut	5 7 8/10	Small scar in the forehead over the right eye. Scar on the middle finger of the right hand. Small scar on the left hand between forefinger and thumb. Born in the County of Northampton State of Virginia (dd)

No	Age	Name	Color	Stature ft inch	Apparent Marks or Scars on Face, Head or Hands
154	About 44yrs Old	James Cottrell	Chesnut	5 11	Scar of considerable size over the left eyebrow. The middle finger on the right hand crooked.
					Born in the County of Northampton State of Virginia (dd)
155	About 26yrs Old	Elizabeth Cottrell	Light Chesnut	5 3	Large scar on the right cheek near the ear. Dark scar from a burn on the back of the right hand
					Born in the County of Northampton State of Virginia (dd)
156	Born in or about 1815	Keziah Becket	Dark Chesnut	4 11 1/2	Several small moles on the cheeks.
					Born in the County of Northampton State of Virginia (dd)
157	Aug 1st 1838	Ann Stockley	Chesnut	5 6	A mole on the fore & one on the middle finger of the right hand. Two or three small moles on the right cheek.
					Born in the County of Northampton State of Virginia (dd)
158	29yrs Old Jun 30th 1859	Tamer Carter	Dark	5 3	A small scar in the middle of the forehead-Thick lips.
					Born in the County of Northampton State of Virginia (dd)
159	39yrs Old Jan 1st 1860	Fannie Collins	Dark Chesnut	5 5	Small mole on the right of the face near the mouth
					Born in the County of Northampton State of Virginia (dd)
160	26yrs Old 20th Mar 1859	Wm Becket	Yellow	5 7 1/2	Several small marks or scars on fore finger of right hand-Wart under the right eye.
					Born in the County of Northampton State of Virginia (dd)

No	Age	Name	Color	Stature ft inch	Apparent Marks or Scars on Face, Head or Hands
161	About 60 yrs 1859	Susan Stephens	Dark Chesnut	5 4 4/10	face full of small black moles.
					Born in the County of Northampton State of Virginia (dd)
162	Mar 19th 1821	Jack Stephens	Black	5 9	Long scar in the middle of the forehead. The nail of the thumb on the left hand has a black mark the entire length of the nail.
					Born in the County of Northampton State of Virginia (dd)
163	Mar 4th 1820	Peter Becket	Chesnut	5 6 4/10	Scar on forehead, one scar in right eye brow. Holes in ears for rings Scar in palm of right hand. Scar on middle finger of right hand.
					Born in the County of Northampton State of Virginia (dd)
164	23yrs Old Jan 7th 1860	Mary Weeks	Chesnut	5 3 4/10	Scar on the right side of the forehead; Mole on the right side of the mouth, The ring finger on the right hand crooked.
					Born in the County of Northampton State of Virginia (dd)
165	17yrs 15th Mar 1859	Maria Moses	Chesnut	5 3 7/10	Holes in ears for rings
					Born in the County of Northampton State of Virginia (dd)
166	30yrs Aug 8th 1860	Elizabeth Cottrell Sr.	Chesnut	5 3	Small scar over the right eye; one over the left eye; The first joint of the middle finger on the right hand____ by a bone_____. Two small Two small scars on the back of the right hand.
					Born in the County of Northampton State of Virginia (dd)
167	Born in the year 1831	Burley Stephens	Chesnut	5 5	Open countenance-small mole on the cheek-and a mole on the back of the right hand.
					Born in the County of Northampton State of Virginia (dd)

No	Age	Name	Color	Stature ft inch	Apparent Marks or Scars on Face, Head or Hands
168	22yrs Old 2nd 1859	James Church	Dark Yellow	5 6 6/10	Small scar on the right cheek bone; Small scar on the right of the nose near the eye, Long Scar on the middle finger of the right hand. Two scars on the left hand near the wrist. Born in the County of Northampton State of Virginia (dd)
169	23yrs Old 1st Sept 1859	Louisa Collins	Black	5 1	Scar on the nose between the eyes; one scar on lip; Scar on left hand between thumb and fore finger-The butter teeth are separated by a small space. Born in the County of Northampton State of Virginia (dd)
170	20th Jun 1822	Edward Weeks	Black	5 10 9/10	One Scar on the forehead one Scar on the left hand Oblong face. Born in the County of Northampton State of Virginia (dd)
171	37yrs Old Apr 1860	Lavinia Weeks	Chesnut	5 4 4/10	Large mole near the nose on the left of the face. Large scar on the left wrist. Scar in the middle of the forehead Born in the County of Northampton State of Virginia (dd)
172	26yrs Aug 10th 1859	Daniel Giddens	Light black	5 8 7/10	Small scar on the back of left hand hand near the fore finger-A scar on the left thumb. Born in the County of Northampton State of Virginia (dd)
173	28yrs Feb 28th 1859	Esther Weeks	Dark Chesnut	5 5 3/10	Long scar on right elbow-Long scar on left arm-Long scar in the palm of the left hand near the wrist. Born in the County of Northampton State of Virginia (dd)
174	22yrs Feb 1860	William Howell	Black	5 4 1/2	No mark on the head or face-Two small scars on he back of the left Small scar on the back of the right hand. Born in the County of Northampton State of Virginia (dd)

No	Age	Name	Color	Stature ft inch	Apparent Marks or Scars on Face, Head or Hands
175	14th Apr 1832	Samuel Carter	Black	5 9	Prominent brow, low forehead, high cheek bones, a scar about three quarters of an inch long in the middle of the forehead, and several little scars on the back of the right hand.
					Born in the County of Northampton State of Virginia (dd)
176	May 6th 1803	Abel Church	Dark Yellow	5 11 4/10	Large Scar on the top of bald head, Scar on the right thumb, The small & ring finger on the left hand deformed.
					Born in the County of Northampton State of Virginia (dd)
177	26yrs Old 15th Aug 1859	Mary Church	Yellow	5 6 2/10	Scar on the end of forefinger of right hand. Small scar on back of right hand, small mole on wrist left hand, small mole on lip, small scar on right cheek
					Born in the County of Northampton State of Virginia (dd)
178	Jun 4th 1806	Bethany Becket Chesnut	Dark	5 3	Scar near the left wrist, Several small moles on the face-
					Born in the County of Accomack State of Virginia (dd)
179	19yrs Aug 1859	Esther Poulson	Light Chesnut	4 6 8/10	Small scar on the back of the right hand between the middle & fore finger Scar on the left fore finger.
					Born in the County of Northampton State of Virginia (dd)
180	Sept 1837	George Burton	Yellow	5 3 4/10	Small scars on little finger of the right hand, several small scars on back of the left hand, scar from burn on right cheek, scar near left eye from burn, small scar in the ___ of the left ear.
					Born in the County of Northampton State of Virginia (dd)
181	Jan 1824	Mary Burton	Chesnut	4 10	Small scar on the forehead, A mole on the right of the face near the nose, small scar on the arm near the place for bleeding- small scar on the left hand on the joint of the thumb.
					Born in the County of Northampton State of Virginia (dd)

No	Age	Name	Color	Stature ft inch	Apparent Marks or Scars on Face, Head or Hands
182	30yrs Old Mar 30th 1859	Mary Roan	Dark Chesnut	4 9 1/2	Scar on the upper lip-Scar over the left eye.
					Born in the County of Northampton State of Virginia (dd)
183	35yrs Old Mar 1859	William Drighouse	Yellow	5 9 9/10	Scar over the right eye about 1/2 inch long and ____ Scar on the right thumb and right fore finger.
					Born in the County of Northampton State of Virginia (dd)
184	21yrs Old Oct 24th 1859	Esther Giddens	Black	4 10 8/10	Scar on the left thumb 2 d Joint- Scar on the right arm near the wrist.
					Born in the County of Northampton State of Virginia (dd)
185	20yrs Old 30th 1859	George Weeks	Dark Chesnut	5 9 4/10	Scar on the left eye brow. Scar at the end of the middle finger of the left hand
					Born in the County of Northampton State of Virginia (dd)
186	25yrs Old 1st Dec 1859	Mary Morris	Chesnut	5 6 3/10	Mole in right ear-mole on forehead. Holes in ears for rings.
					Born in the County of Northampton State of Virginia (dd)
187	17th Feb 1814	Leah White	Bacon	5 1 7/10	Small scar over the right eye. Small Small scar on the right arm near the wrist. Small scar on the back of the of the left hand.
					Emancipated by deed from Teackle White recorded in the Clerk's Office of the County of Northampton the 15th day of April A. D. 1806
					No notation was made as to permission to reside in the State of Virginis or County of Northampton.

No	Age	Name	Color	Stature ft inch	Apparent Marks or Scars on Face, Head or Hands
188	Born in or about 1809	Belle Pitts	Very Black	5 4	Long woolly hair, open space between front upper teeth, oval face, one scar on the back of left hand.
					Emancipated at the age of twenty five years by the will of John Pitts dec. recorded in Northampton county Court the 8th March 1819.
					Permission has not been granted to Belle Pitts reside in this State-
189	18yrs Old 15th Jan 1860	Elizabeth Stephens	Black	4 11 3/10	Large scar on neck just below the chin-several small scars on back of right hand.
					Born in the County of Northampton State of Virginia (dd)
190	Born in or about 1825	Mary Ann Stephens	Black	5 2	Scar on left cheek, Holes in ears for rings, Scar under the thumb of the right hand.
					Born in the County of Northampton State of Virginia (dd)
191	26th Jan 1814	Leah Pitts	Dark Chesnut	5 3	Small darkish mole on back of neck, mole near left ear and temple
					Emancipated at the age of 25 years by the will of John Pitts decd., recorded in Northampton County Cout on the 8th day of April 1819-
					No permission has been granted to Leah Pitts to reside in this State.
192	21yrs Old 20th Aug 1859	John Ames Jr.	dark Chesnut	5 8 1/2	Holes in ears for rings
					Born in the County of Northampton State of Virginia (dd)
193	21yrs Old 27th May 1859	Joshua Simkins	Chesnut	5 7	Scar on fore finger of left hand.
					Born in the County of Northampton State of Virginia (dd)

No	Age	Name	Color	Stature ft inch	Apparent Marks or Scars on Face, Head or Hands
194	40yrs Old 27th Dec 1859	Amy Stephens	Chesnut	5 4 7/10	Holes in ears, mole in palm of left hand Born in the County of Northampton State of Virginia (dd)
195	63yrs Old May 23d 1859	Peter Gleason	Dark Chesnut	5 3 1/2	Scar in the middle of the forehead. End of the little finger on the right hand crooked. Emancipated by the will of Betsy Gleason, recorded in Northampton County Court on the 13th day of January A.D. 1806. No notation appears in the records as to permission for Peter Gleason to reside in the state or county.
196	Born about 1829	Elizabeth Collins	Light Chesnut	5 4 8/10	A small scar on left of right eye, scar on right wrist underneath of wrist. Born in the County of Northampton State of Virginia. (dd)
197	20yrs Old 18th Jan	Margaret Stephens Jr.	Light Chesnut	5 6/10	Scar on the knuckle of the middle finger left hand- Scar on back of right hand, Scar on inside of right arm-Holes in ears for rings. Born in the County of Northampton State of Virginia (dd)
198	25th Nov 1805	Dinah Stephens	Dark Black	5 3 8/10	Oblong face, thin hair, scar in middle of the forehead, a scar on right side of neck, small black mole on inside of left arm. Born in the County of Northampton State of Virginia (dd)
199	23yrs Old Aug 5th 1859	Mary Upshur	Light Chesnut	5 1/2	Small scar on the left hand near root of the thumb, also on the first joint of the thumb. Born in the County of Northampton State of Virginia (dd)

No	Age	Name	Color	Stature ft inch	Apparent Marks or Scars on Face, Head or Hands
200	21yrs Old 25th Aug 1859	Leah Church	Yellow	5 /10	Scar on inside of right wrist, caused by burn-Scar on little finger of right hand-;finger next to little finger of right hand cut off at second joint.
					Born in the County of Northampton State of Virginia (dd)
201	39yrs Old 10th Jun 1859	Rachel Howell	Black	5 2 3/10	Little crosseyed-the two upper teeth are out-
					Born in the County of Northampton State of Virginia (dd)
202	37yrs Old Sept 14th 1859	Ann Collins	Yellow	5 5 1/2	Small scar on the chin-Mole over the right eye. Small scar at the root of the right thumb
					Born in the County of Northampton State of Virginia (dd)
203	19yrs Old Jan 6th 1860	Sarah Collins	Yellow	5 5 8/10	No marks or scars on the face. Several moles on the face. One prominent mole on the left of the face near the mouth. Scar on the left hand near the thumb. Scar on the left hand near the fore finger.
					Born in the County of Northampton State of Virginia (dd)
204	65yrs Old 15th Nov 1859	Maria Collins	Chesnut	5 6 2/10	Scar on right side of neck, 2 scars on back of right hand.
					Born in the County of Northampton State of Virginia (dd)
205	21yrs 10th May 1859	Griffin Collins Jr	Yellow	5 8	Small scar on forehead.
					Born in the County of Northampton State of Virginia (dd)

No	Age	Name	Color	Stature ft inch	Apparent Marks or Scars on Face, Head or Hands
206	1828	Abram Stevens	Black	5 10 9/10	Small scar near the corner of right eye; high forehead; scar on the middle knuckle of the left fore finger. Born in the County of Northampton State of Virginia (dd)
207	25yrs Old 25th Jan 1859	John Wesley Onley	Mulatto	5 10 9/10	Scar in the palm of right hand. Born in the County of Northampton State of Virginia (dd)
208	21yrs Old Jun 1859	Henry Webb	Chesnut	5 11 3/10	Small scar on the right hand between the wrist & thumb, small scar on the back of right hand; Scar on the back of left hand near the fore finger. Born in the County of Northampton State of Virginia (dd)
209	24yrs Next Jan (1860)	Damary Matthews	Chesnut	4 10 /12	Enlargement of the left ear, Mole in the right ear. Enlargement of the middle finger at the end. Long scar on the left hand between the thumb and fore finger. Born in the County of Northampton State of Virginia (dd)
210	20yrs Nov last (1859)	Laura Harmon	Light Chesnut	5 4 7/10	Small scar over the left eye. Two small moles over the left eye. No marks or scars on the hands. Born in the County of Northampton State of Virginia (dd)
211	24yrs last Aug 15th 1859)	James Harman	Yellow	5 4 4/10	Mole on the left side of the face near the ear-Little finger on right hand straight, cannot be crooked in either the first or second joint- caused by a cut on the inside of the right hand near the thumb joint. Born in the County of Northampton State of Virginia (dd)

No	Age	Name	Color	Stature ft inch	Apparent Marks or Scars on Face, Head or Hands
212	25yrs Mar 1859	Bridget Drighouse	Light Chesnut	5 4 3/10	Two scars on the forehead, Scars on on each ear caused by holes for rings. Scar on the left hand near the wrist Scar on the back of the right hand between the fore and middle finger. Born in the County of Northampton State of Virginia (dd)
213	28yrs 2d. Sept 1859	Ellen Brickhouse	Light Chesnut	5 3/10	Mole on left cheek Born in the County of Northampton State of Virginia (dd)
214	25yrs Oct 15th 1859	Elizabeth Becket	Light Chesnut	4 10	Small scar on the back of left hand. No scars on the face or head. Born in the County of Accomack State of Virginia (dd)
215	20yrs Jul 22d. 1859	Margaret Becket	Chesnut	4 11 9/10	No marks or scars on the face or Face bumpy, Scar on the right wrist. Born in the County of Northampton State of Virginia (dd)
216	Sept 1813	Leah Becket	Light Chesnut	4 9 1/2	Flesh mole at the end of the right nostril-two small moles on the right cheek. Hair inclined to be straight-The upper front teeth are out. Born in the County of Northampton State of Virginia (dd)
217	Aug 10th 1818	John Becket of Abram	Yellow	5 5 1/2	Oblong face, high and receding forehead, lively expression of countenance Born in the County of Northampton State of Virginia (dd)

No	Age	Name	Color	Stature ft inch	Apparent Marks or Scars on Face, Head or Hands
218	Dec 25th 1821	Patience Stephens	Light Mulatto	5 5	Scar on the left temple-Straight black hair-Scar on the ring finger of the right hand, at the end, caused by a bone felon. Born in the County of Northampton State of Virginia (dd)
219	Feb 1st 1842	Kitty Stephens	Very light Mulatto	5 4 1/2	Mole on the neck-a small mole on each cheek.-Scar on the ring finger of the right hand, near the nail. Amiable expression of countenance. Born in the County of Northampton State of Virginia (dd)
220	Mar 10th 1821	Levin Moses	Light Chesnut	5 7 3/10	Scar on the nose between the eyes; Scar on the chin-two scars on the back of the left hand. Born in the County of Northampton State of Virginia (dd)
221	1802	Isaac Kendall	Chesnut	5 8 1/5	oblong face-Scar on the left hand at the top joint of the little finger- The right ear is deformed. Born in the County of Northampton State of Virginia (dd)
222	May 1807	Luke Trower	Bright Mulatto	5 8 1/2	Small dark scar on the left corner of the right eye-a small scar near the middle of the forehead, a little to the left side; holes in ears for rings. Born in the County of Northampton State of Virginia (dd)
223	Mar 15th 1804	Solomon Matthews	Black	5 10 3/10	Small scar on the left end of the left eye brow; small scar on the right temple. Scar near the knuckle of the left fore finger of the left hand. Born in the County of Northampton State of Virginia (dd)
224	May 17th 1847	Henrietta Williams	Black	5 1	Scar on the nose at the corner of the left eye. Very small scar on the back of the right hand. Born in the County of Northampton State of Virginia (dd)

No	Age	Name	Color	Stature ft inch	Apparent Marks or Scars on Face, Head or Hands
225	May 20th 1840	Louisa Thompson	Black	5　5 3/10	Scar between the eyes, some small scars on the forehead, and some small scars on the right temple from the effects of chicken pox. Mole in the palm of the left hand. Born in the County of Northampton State of Virginia (dd)
226	Dec 4th 1837	William Onley	Mulatto	5　7 1/5	Small mole on the left cheek-thick hair-a very small mole on the middle finger of the left hand. Born in the County of Northampton State of Virginia (dd)
227	20th Sept 1824	William Stephens	Chesnut	5　7 6/10	Scar at corner of left eye brow 3/4 inch long-scar on back of left hand-Small wen on left wrist. Born in the County of Northampton State of Virginia (dd)
228	25yrs Mar 17th 1860	Jane Becket	Dark Yellow	5　2 2/10	No marks or scars on the face or head or head-Small scar on right fore finger of the right hand. Scar near the nail of the ring finger of the left hand. Very large upper front teeth. Born in the County of Northampton State of Virginia (dd)
229	Jun 15th 1828	Solomon Church	Chesnut	5　7	Long narrow face, high forehead-mole on the under lid of the left eye. Scar on the fleshy part of the right hand between the thumb and fore finger. Born in the County of Northampton State of Virginia (dd)
230	Aug 4th 1817	Samuel Bevans	Black	5　5 8/10	Scar just in front of the right ear-about three inches long. Mole on the inside of the middle finger of the left hand. Born in the County of Northampton State of Virginia (dd)
231	Jan 22 1825	Matilda Bevans	Light Chesnut	5　2 8/10	Round face and good expression of of countenance. Small black mole of the chin. Born in the County of Northampton State of Virginia (dd)

No	Age	Name	Color	Stature ft inch	Apparent Marks or Scars on Face, Head or Hands
232	Aug 12th 1813	Mary Guy	Yellow	5 4	Several marks on the nose and face from the effects of small pox; two small moles on the left cheek. Born in the County of Northampton State of Virginia (dd)
233	Mar 4th 1817	Emeline Jacob	Light Chesnut	5 4 1/2	Some very small moles on the right two small moles in the palm of the right hand-scar about an inch long in the palm of the right hand. Born in the County of Northampton State of Virginia (dd)
234	Jan 31st 1841	Louisa Rozell	Light Chesnut	5 1 1/2	High cheek bones, small scar on each cheek; small eyes and short teeth. Born in the County of Northampton State of Virginia (dd by mail Feb. 1860 to Franktown)
235	Jan 22d 1829	Jacob Church	Dark Chesnut	5 9 8/10	Scar on the upper part of the nose between the eyes; scar near the corner of the left eye. Born in the County of Northampton State of Virginia (dd)
236	Mar 13th 1827	Littleton Church	Dark Chesnut	6 0 1/4	Scar on the upper lip-small scar on the fore finger of the left hand-oblong face-Hair grows well down the forehead. Born in the County of Northampton State of Virginia dd May 12.'60
237	Mar 8th 1829	Severn Stevens	Black	5 3	High cheek bones, small scar on the left cheek. Knuckle of the left thumb enlarged; scar on the inner part of the middle finger of the left hand. Born in the County of Northampton State of Virginia dd May 12, '60

No	Age	Name	Color	Stature ft inch	Apparent Marks or Scars on Face, Head or Hands
238	No Date Given	Amy Savage	Chesnut	5 6 1/2	Small scar at the upper end of the nose & between the eyebrows; small mole on the right nostril, and one just below the same nostril.
					Emancipated by the last Will and Testament of Arthur R. Savage, deceased, Recorded in the clerk's office of Northampton County Court on the 13th day of February 1837.
					Permission has not been granted to Amy Savage to reside in the State by the Northampton County Court. dd to L. D. H.

111 Registers-year ending Aug. 31, 1860

No	Age	Name	Color	Stature ft inch	Apparent Marks or Scars on Face, Head or Hands
239	Sept 1839	Sabra B. Catt	Dark Chesnut	5 3 1/2	Small mole near the left ear. Scar on the right temple. Small scar on back of right hand.
					Born in the County of Northampton State of Virginia dd to L. D. H.
240	Dec 16th 1837	Mary A. Catt	Black	5 2	Mole in the palm of the left hand. Scar under tahe right eye.
					Born in the County of Northampton State of Virginia dd to L. D. H.
241	Dec 1828	Ann Collins	Light Chesnut	5 5 1/2	Mole on the left cheek; small moles on the right cheek; several small moles under the left eye.
					Born in the County of Northampton State of Virginia
242	14yrs 9th Dec 1860	Maria J. Weeks	Chesnut	5 1 3/10	A small scar near the root of the the right ear.
					Born in the County of Northampton State of Virginia (dd)
243	Born in the fall of 1817	William Becket of Rachel	Chesnut	5 6 1/2	Scar above the brow of the right eye; round full forehead; scar on the wrist of the right hand.
					Born in the County of Accomack State of Virginia (dd)

No	Age	Name	Color	Stature ft inch	Apparent Marks or Scars on Face, Head or Hands
244	Born 1794 Born on Christmas	Nelson Churches	Black	5 7	Two scars under the right eye, Scar on the forehead. Oblong face.
					Emancipated by deed from John Upshur, Sr., Recorded in Northampton County Court Dec 9th, 1799.
					Permission not needed if emancipated before 1806
245	Born 1839	Susan Collins	Light Chesnut	4 1 2/5	Scar at the right corner of the right eye; small scar on the rightcheek; Small scar on the fore finger of the right hand.
					Born in the County of Northampton State of Virginia (dd) By mail, to J.E.N.
246	Born 1820	Emeline Cottrell	Light Chesnut	5 3	Scar on the back of left hand; two moles on on left cheek and one on the right cheek. Thin visage.
					Born in the County of Northampton State of Virginia (dd) By mail, to J.E.N.
247	Born Apr 1831	Mary Ann Stephens	Mulatto	5 2 3/10	Scar in the middle of the forehead; scar on he wrist of the right hand.
					Born in the County of Northampton State of Virginia (dd)
248	Born 25th May 1782	Esther Collins	Yellow	5 4 1/2	Scar on the inside of the under lip; several several small moles on each side of the face.
					Born in the County of Northampton State of Virginia (dd)
249	Born 18th Mar 1808	Roxaline Collins	Mulatto	5 1 1/2	Small mole on the under lid of the right eye; ring hole on the left ear torn out, and a scar there from. Scar on the third joint of the left fore finger on the inner side.
					Born in the County of Northampton State of Virginia (dd)
250	Born Sept 22nd 1811	Mary Matthews	Light Black	5 1	Small mole under left eye; Small mole just in front of the left ear. Some small moles on left cheek. Middle finger of the left hand crooked, so that it cannot be straightened.
					Born in the County of Northampton State of Virginia (dd)

No	Age	Name	Color	Stature ft inch	Apparent Marks or Scars on Face, Head or Hands
251	Born Oct 1830	James Rozelle	Chesnut	5 7 1/2	Round face; two small scars on the left cheek Scar on the back of right hand at the knuckle of middle finger. Born in the County of Northampton State of Virginia (dd) By mail to J. E. N.
252	Born 10th Aug 1822	Isaac Reed	Chesnut	5 8 1/2	Scar just above the brow of the right eye; Scar across the upper or small part of the nose Born in the County of Northampton State of Virginia (dd)
253	Born 1833	Nathaniel Sutton	Black	4 7 1/2	Broad face, flat nose, good forehead, thick lips, scar on the forehead just above the right eye brow. Born in the County of Northampton State of Virginia (dd)
254	Born Aug 11th 1839	Sally Ann Simkins	Chesnut	5 0	Slight scar on the left cheek; small scar on the wrist of the right hand. Born in the County of Northampton State of Virginia (dd)
255	Born Sept 20th 1834	Tamar Simkins	Yellow	5 5 1/2	Front teeth defective; Scar on left hand near the thumb; scar on back of right hand. Born in the County of Northampton State of Virginia (dd)
256	Born 14th Apr 1843	George Avery Simkins	Chesnut	5 2 1/2	Naked place on the back part of head; Horizontal scar in the middle of forehead; Scar on the Left hand. Born in the County of Northampton State of Virginia (dd)
257	Born May 1st 1841	Esther Pitts	Yellow	5 1 1/2	Several frackles on the nose and each cheek. Scar on the neck and two moles on the same Descendent of Leah Pitts emancipated by the will of John Pitts, recorded in Northampton County Court the 8th day of March 1819. [permission] Not granted by the Court of Northampton. Born in the County of Northampton State of Virginia (dd)

No	Age	Name	Color	Stature ft inch	Apparent Marks or Scars on Face, Head or Hands
258	Born Nov 7th 1812	Abel Francis	Mulatto	5 7 1/2	Straight black hair; grey eyes, small scar on the right cheek, and some small scars on the fore and middle fingers of right hand.
					Born in the County of Northampton State of Virginia (dd)
259	Born 18th Mar 1833	Polly Francis	Yellow	5 3	One front tooth out-Small scar on brow of right eye. Blue eyes. Small scar under the left eye.
					Born in the County of Northampton State of Virginia (dd)
260	Born July 18th 1839	Sally Francis	Yellow	5 3 1/3	Dark scar on the left wrist. Small scar on the right hand near the root of the thumb.
					Born in the County of Northampton State of Virginia (dd)
261	Born Mar 1830	Arinthia Stephens	Chesnut	5 5 1/5	Scar on the right cheek; and a small round scar on the right wrist.
					Born in the County of Northampton State of Virginia (dd)
262	Born Jan 1834	William Brickhouse	Yellow	5 7 7/10	Scar under the right eye, scar on the left cheek; Mole under the left eye; Scar on left little finger.
					Born in the County of Northampton State of Virginia (dd)
263	Born Sept 13th 1840	Dennis Cottrell	Chesnut	5 7 7/10	A mole on the left of the face near the mouth; Scars on the fore, middle and ring finger.
					Born in the County of Northampton State of Virginia (dd)
264	Born Aug 2nd 1839	Lloyd Wm. Jacob Jacob	Chesnut	5 6 8/10	Oblong face; Scar just under the right eye; some small scars on the back of each hand.
					Born in the County of Northampton State of Virginia (dd)

No	Age	Name	Color	Stature ft inch	Apparent Marks or Scars on Face, Head or Hands
265	Born May 16th 1813	George Simkins	Black	5 6 1/2	Scar on the back of left hand. Blind in the left eye.
					Born in the County of Northampton State of Virginia (dd)
266	Born Mar 1824	Harriet Scisco	Light Chesnut	5 6	Round full face; some small moles on each cheek.
					Born in the County of Northampton State of Virginia (dd)
267	Born Oct 13th 1815	Henry Scisco	Black	5 7 1/2	Bald from forehead to crown of head; Scar over right eye brow near the temple
					Born in the County of Northampton State of Virginia (dd)
268	Born Oct 1840	Custis Howell	Black	5 4 6/10	Low narrow forehead, a small scar in the middle of forehead; Scar on back of left hand; small mole on right cheek.
					Born in the County of Northampton State of Virginia (dd)
269	Born 1833 Mar 20th	Mary Stephens	Yellow	5 2 1/2	Scar on the left hand; Face very much freckled on each cheek below the eyes.
					Born in the County of Northampton State of Virginia (dd)
270	Born Sept 10th	Christopher Collins	Yellow	5 3 6/10	Scar on the joint of the left thumb; Scars on forehead, one near the left eye brow and the other above the right eye brow
					Born in the County of Northampton State of Virginia (dd)
271	Born 1830	Custis Morris	Dark Chesnut	5 7	Small scar on the left cheek below nostril. Scar on back of right hand; Scar on fore finger of left hand.
					Born in the County of Northampton State of Virginia (dd)

No	Age	Name	Color	Stature ft inch	Apparent Marks or Scars on Face, Head or Hands
272	Born Aug 22d. 1833	John Stephens	Yellow	5 8	Scar between the eyebrows two small moles on of right hand; some small moles on the face.
					Born in the County of Northampton State of Virginia (dd)
273	Born Mar 27th 1836	Louisa Upshur	Chesnut	5 6 8/10	Mole between the eye brows, also a mole on the nose; small mole near the right nostril. Scar on the back of left hand.
					Born in the County of Northampton State of Virginia (dd)
274	Born 1847	Victor C. Collins	Yellow	4 8 1/2	Straight black hair, two small moles on the left cheek; a small round scar at the right end of right eyebrow.
					Born in the County of Northampton State of Virginia (dd)
275	Born Mar 10th 1833	George Poulson	Chesnut	5 6	Scar at the right end of the right eye brow; Scar on left nostril. Scar on the right fore finger.
					Born in the County of Northampton State of Virginia (dd)
276	Born May 1819	Francis Asberry Morris	Chesnut	5 3 9/10	There seems to be no apparent marks or scars. Open countanance; tolerable wide mouth, Prominent brow; High forehead, Scar at the end of the ring finger of the right hand.
					Born in the County of Northampton State of Virginia (dd)
277	Born Apr 2nd 1826	Betsy Rozell	Yellow	5 6 1/2	Scar near the right nostril, Scar over the left eye; and a scar under the left eye.
					Born in the County of Northampton State of Virginia (dd)
278	Born Mar 18th 1841	Wesley Francis	Yellow	5 7 1/2	Small scar about one fourth of an inch long near the left eye.
					Born in the County of Northampton State of Virginia (dd)

No	Age	Name	Color	Stature ft inch	Apparent Marks or Scars on Face, Head or Hands
279	Born Nov 12th 1842	Edna Francis	Yellow	5 2	Small scar under the chin on the left side; Small scar near the nose and under the left eye; Small scar on the left thumb. Born in the County of Northampton State of Virginia (dd)
280	Born Dec 25th 1840	Stokely Morris	Chesnut	5 9 1/2	Scar on left side of forehead near the hair; Scar on the left cheek; Some small scars on the back of left hand. Born in the County of Northampton State of Virginia (dd)
281	Born Jun 8th 1818	Leah Brickhouse	Mulatto	5 5 8/10	Large prominent eyes, oval face; high forehead. Born in the County of Northampton State of Virginia (dd)
282	Born July 1827	Caleb Collins	Chesnut	5 7 1/2	A small scar near the left eye; A scar near the left temple. Scar on the left thumb at the end. Born in the County of Northampton State of Virginia (dd)
283	Born Sept 1834	Sabra Collins	Yellow	5 3 1/2	A small scar on the left side of the neck. A small scar on the left wrist. Born in the County of Northampton State of Virginia
284	Born about 1818	Margaret Harmon	Mulatto	5 0 1/2	Scar on the forehead over the left eye; Small scar near the wrist of the right hand. Born in the County of Northampton State of Virginia (dd)
285	Born Dec 3rd 1845	Lavinia Ellen Weeks	Chesnut	5 4 8/10	Small scar on the left fore finger. Large long scar on the left arm between the elbow & wrist. Born in the County of Northampton State of Virginia (dd)

No	Age	Name	Color	Stature ft inch	Apparent Marks or Scars on Face, Head or Hands
286	Born Apr 1847	Frances Sarah Weeks	Chesnut	5 1 1/10	Two small scars in the middle of the forehead. Born in the County of Northampton State of Virginia (dd)
287	Born Jan 21st 1821	Mary Ames	Black	5 5	Scar on the back of left hand crossing the knuckle of the middle finger; Scar on the left ear; small round scar near the right temple; Small scar on the left cheek. Born in the County of Northampton State of Virginia (dd)
288	Born Sept 22nd	William Webb	Chesnut	5 9	Scar on the right ear; scar on the ring finger of the right hand near the back knuckle. Born in the County of Northampton State of Virginia (dd)
289	Born Oct 25th 1834	Abel Church Jr	Light Chesnut	5 8 4/10	Small scar just under the nose, and a scar on the left cheek Born in the County of Northampton State of Virginia (dd)
290	Born Dec 5th 1833	Henry Collins	Yellow	5 4	Small scar on the right cheek, Scar on the left thumb; S mole on the forehead. Born in the County of Northampton State of Virginia (dd)
291	Born 1840	Mary Ann Church	Chesnut	5 2 1/2	Scar on the left wrist, and also a small scar on the right wrist. Born in the County of Northampton State of Virginia (dd)
292	16yrs Old 31st Mar 1860	Margaret Brickhouse	Yellow	5 3 6/10	A very small scar over the right eye; A mole on the right of the nose & a mole and a mole on the left cheek, A small scar on the right wrist. Born in the County of Northampton State of Virginia (dd)

No	Age	Name	Color	Stature ft inch	Apparent Marks or Scars on Face, Head or Hands
293	Born Dec 25th 1828	George Stephens	Black	5 7	Scar on the right cheek; holes in ears for for rings, the one in the right ear is torn out; two small scars on the left eye brow. Born in the County of Northampton State of Virginia (dd)

55 Registers to Aug 31, 1861

APPENDIX I

Register of Free Negroes
Order Book 39, 1831-1836
Page 18

It is ordered to be certified that the registers of Jeptha Barcroft, Mary Bevans (wife of John), Mary Bevans (wife of Sam), Sukey Bailey, George Baker, Elizabeth Baker, Judah Baker, Mary Baker, Betsy Baker, Comfort Baker, Jane Bevans, Sam Bevans Jr, Thomas Bevans, Rachel Bevans, Thomas Bevans Sen, Thomas Bevans Jr, Nancy Bevans, Mary Bevans, Isaac Becket, Sukey Becket, Margaret Becket, Maria Becket, Peggy Becket, Sally Becket (formerly Sally Stephens), Sally Becket, Solomon Becket, Elizabeth Becket, Betsy Becket, Robert I. Bingham, Lucretia Bingham, Thamar Bingham, Adah Bradford, Esther Brickhouse, Abel Brickhouse, Benjamin Brickhouse, Comfort Brickhouse, Ben Carter, Betsy Carter, Thamar Carter, Edy Carter, Rachel Christian, Abel Church, James Church, Lucy Church (formerly Lucy Thompson), Toney Church, Eliza Churches, Milly Churches, Nicy Churches, Peter Churches, Comfort Churches, Betsy Collins, Betsy Collins (formerly Betsy Stephens), Charlotte Collins, Custis Collins, Eliza Collins, Eliza Collins Jr, Fanny Collins, Fanny Collins (little), Jacob Collins, John Collins (of Lighty), Mary Collins, Demary Collins (alias Demary Jeffery), Major Collins, Nancy Collins, Margaret Collins, Peggy Collins (JT), Peggy Collins (FT), Priscilla Collins, Rosy Collins, Roxaline Collins, Winney Collins, Comfort Collins, Comfort Jr, Elcerna Cropper, Betty Drighouse, Rosy Drighouse, Polly Drighouse, Sally Drighouse, Leah Dunton, Thomas Francis Sen, Peggy Francis, Teackle Francis, Harriet Giddens, Comfort Giddens, Sarah Giddens, Louisa Giddens, Jacob Gustin, Sarah Gusten, Esther Guy, Abel Hartney, Esther Hampton, George Harman, Adah Howell, Mary Howell, Nancy Howell, Nancy Jeffery (formerly Nancy Collins), Annie Johnson, Thamar Johnson, Benjamin Johnson, Bridget Judah, Rachel Kellam, Charlotte Lang, Phillis Lang, Tinney Lang, Mary Lang (alias Mary West), Betsy Lang, Betsy Lewis, George Lewis, Littleton Major, Wm Major, Rosy Major, Levi Matthews, Rebecca Matthews, Solomon Matthews, Jesse Milby, Michael Morris, Henry Morris, Rosana Morris, Jack Perkins (alias Jack Pettit), George Pitts (alias George Toney), Betsy Pool, Hessy Pool, Mary Ann Pool, Rosy Pool, Jenny Pool, Ann Pool, Ben Powell, William Powell, Betsy Powell, Eliza Press, Dinah Read, Betsy Read, Betsy Read Jr, Jacob Read, William Roberts, Jack Rose, Jinny Roward, Nicey Roward, John Sample, Sally Sample (formerly Sally Morris), Rosy Sample, James Satchell, Mary Satchell, Harriet Scisco, Major Scisco, Peter Simkins, Milly Simkins, Betsy Upshur, Betsy Stephens Jr., Betsy Stephens (formerly Betsy Thompson), Caroline Stephens, Eliza Stephens, Harry Stephens, Isaac Stephens, Leah Stephens, Mary Stephens (wife of GW), Mary Stephens (alias Mary Haitney), Peggy Stephens, Rachell Stephens, Sabra Stephens (formerly Sabra Nutts), Susan Stephens, Henry Stephens, Peggy Stephens, Lucy Stephens, Rachel Stephens, Bridget Thompson, Margaret Thompson, Mary Thompson, Louisa Toyer (alias Louisa Bevans), Susy Toyer (alias Susy Pool), Bethany Trower, Catherine Webb, Isaac Webb, John Webb, Levin Webb Sen, Levin Webb Jr, Rachel Webb, James West, Mary West, Mahala West, Leah Whittington, Betsy Wickes, Comfort Wickes, James Wickes, Mary Wickes, Nancy Wickes, Spencer Wickes, Mary Ann Wickes, Sam Wooser, Free Negroes are truly made.

Order that this court be adjourned until tomorrow morning at ten O'clock.

Addison

APPENDIX II

NOTES ABOUT WILLS AND VIRGINIA LAWS
Spelling, Punctuation, and Abbreviation

All wills were transcribed from the original wills located in various Will Books in the Clerk's Office of Northampton County, Virginia. The Virginia laws were also transcribed without correction from Virginia Laws 1661 to 1865. The laws were recorded on microfiche and located in the Brooklyn, New York Law Library. The spelling, punctuations, abbreviations and phrases were transcribed just as they appear in the original form. There are several peculiarities in the spellings, punctuations and abbreviations that we have noted here.

The following represent consistent spelling differences:

allsoe	also
appoynt	appoint
authorise	authorize
bee	be
captayne	captain
compleat	complete
conteying	containing
dew	due
doe	do
fyled	filed
fowerteen	fourteen
graunted	granted
moneth	month
ofspring	offspring
publique	public
remayne	remain
lyable	liable
shew	show
sonne	son
sirname	surname
yeares	years

Punctuation such as periods and commas were not visible in some cases. This may be due to age of the documents. The colon(:) was used as a period sometimes following an abbreviation.

Sd	said		J.P.	Justice of the Peace
afsd	aforesaid		CNC	Clerk Northampton Court
examd	examined		D.C.	Deputy Clerk
Exd	examined		dec'd	deceased
Junr:	Junior		Senr:	Senior
(L.S.)	Legal Seal		Thos	Thomas
Lytt:	Lyttleton		Dew:	Deward

RELEVANT VIRGINIA LAWS

January, 1639
Act X

All persons, except negroes to be provided with arms and ammunition or be fined at pleasure of the Governor and Council.

March, 1659-16
Act XVI
An Act for the Dutch and all other Strangers for Tradeing to this Place

Whereas the restriction of trade hath appeared to be the greatest impediment to the advance of the estimation and value of our present only commodity tobacco, *Be it enacted and confirmed*, That the Dutch and all strnagers of what Xpian nation soever in amity with the people of England shall have free liberty to trade with us, for all allowable comodities. And receive protection from us to our utmost powers while they are in our jurisdiction, and shall have equall right and justice with our own nation in all courts of judicature, Provided they give bond and pay the impost of tenn shillings per hogshead laid upon all tobacco exported to any fforreigne dominious and give bond according to act, *Allwaies provided,* That if the said Dutch or other forreiners shall import any negro slaves, They the said Dutch or others shall, for the tobacco really produced by the sale of the said negro, pay only the impost of two shillings per hogshead, the like being paid by our owne nation.

December, 1662
Act XII
Negro womens children to serve according to the condition of the mother

Whereas some doubts have arrisen whether children got by any Englishman upon a negro woman should be slave or ffree, *Be it therefore enacted and declared* by this present grand assembly, thatt all children borne in this country shalbe held bond or free only according to the condition of the mother, *And* that if any christian shall committ ffornication with a negro man or woman, hee or shee soe offending shall pay double the fines imposed by the former act.

September, 1668
Act VII
Negro women not exempted from tax.

Whereas some doubts, have arisen whether negro women set free were still to be accompted thithable according to a former act, *It is declared by this grand assembly* that negro women, though permitted to enjoy their ffreedome yet ought not in all respects to be admitted to a full fruition of the exemptions and impunities of the English, and are still lyable to payment of taxes.

October, 1670
Act V.
Noe Negroes nor Indians to buy christian servants

Whereas it hath beene questioned whither Indians or negroes manumited, or otherwise free, could be capable of purchasing christian servants. *It is enacted* that noe negroe or Indian though baptised and enjoyned their owne ffreedome shall be capable of any such purchase of christians, but yet not debarred from buying any of their owne nation.

June, 1680
ACT X.
An act for preventing Negroes Insurrections.
Whereas the frequent meeting of considerable numbers of negroe slaves under pretence of feasts and burialls is judged of dangerous consequence; for prevention whereof for the future, Bee it enacted by the kings most excellent majestie by and with the consent of the generall assembly, and it is hereby enacted by the authority

aforesaid, that from and after the publication of this law, it shall not be lawfull for any negroe or other slave to carry or arme himselfe with any club, staffe, gunn, sword or any other weapon of defence, nor to goe or depart from of his masters ground without a certificate from his master, mistris or overseer, and such permission not to be granted but upon perticuler and necessary occasions; and every negroe or slave soe offending not havieing a certificate as aforesaid shalbe sent to the next constable, who is hereby enjoyned and required to give the said negroe twenty lashes on his bare back well layd on, and soe sent home to his said master, mistris or overseer. And it is further enacted by the authority of aforesaid that if any negroe or other slave shall presume to lift up his hand in opposition against any christian, shall for every such offence, upon due proofe made thereof by the oath of the party before a magistrate, have and receive thirty lashes on his bare back well laid on. And it is hereby further enacted by the authority aforesaid that if any negroe or other slave shall absent himself from his masters service and lye hid and lurking in obscure places, comitting injuries to the inhabitants, and shall resis any person or persons that shaby any lawfull authority be imployed to apprehend and take the said negroe, that then in case of such resistance, it shalbe lawfull for such person or persons to kill the said negroe or slave soe lying out and resisting, and that this law be once every six months published at the respective county courts and parish churches within this colony.

November, 1682
Act 1
An act to repeale a former law making Indians and other ffree.

Whereas by the 12 act of assembly held att James Citty the 3d day of October, Anno Domini 1670, entituled an act declareing who shall be slaves, *it is enacted* that all servants not being christians, being imported into this country by shipping shall be slaves, but what shall come by land shall serve if boyes and girls untill thirty yeares of age, if men or women, twelve yeares and noe longer; and for as much as many negroes, moores, mollatoes and others borne of and in heathenish, idollatrous, pagan and mahometan parentage and country have heretofore, and hereafter may be purchased, procured, or otherwise obteigned as slaves, of from or out of such their heathenish country by some well disposed christian, who after such their obteining and purchaseing such negroe, moor, or molatto as their slave out of a pious zeale, have wrought the conversion of such slave to the christian faith, which by the laws of this country doth not manumitt them or make them free, and afterwards such their conversion, it hath and may often happen that such master or owner of such slave being by some reason enforced to bring or send such slave into this country to sell or dispose of for his necessity or advantage, he the said master or owner of such servant which notwithstanding his conversion is really his slave, or his factor or agent must be constrained either to carry back or export againe the said slave to some other place where they may sell him for a slave, or else depart from their just right and tytle to such slave and sell him here for noe longer time then the English or other christians are to serve, to the great losse and damage of such master or owner, and to the great discouragement of being in such slaves for the future, and to noe advantage at all to the planter or buyer; and whereas alsoe those Indians that are take in warre or otherwise by out neighbouring Indians, confederates or atributaries to his majestie, and this his plantation of Virginia are slaves to the said neighbouring Indians that soe take them, and by them are likewise sold to his majesties subjects here as slaves, Bee it therefore enacted by the governour councell and burgesses of this general assembly, and it is enacted by the authority aforesaid, that all the said recited act of the third of october 1670 be, and is hereby repealed and made utterly voyd to all intents and purposes whatsoever. *And be it further enacted* by the authority aforesaid that all servants except Turkes and Moores, whilst in amity with his majesty which from and after publication of this act shall be brought or imported into this country, either by sea or land, whether Negroes, Moors, Mollatttoes or Indians, who and whose parentage and native country are not christian at the time of their first purchase of such servant by some christian although afterwards, and before such their importation and bringing into this country, they shall be converted to the christian faith; and all Indians which shall hereafter be sold by our neighbouring Indians, or any other trafiqueing with us as for slaves are hereby adjudged, deemed and taken, and shall be adjudged, deemed and taken to be slaves to all intents and purposes, any law, usage or custome to the contrary notwithstanding.

November, 1682
Act III
An additionall act for the butter preventing insurrections by Negroes.
Whereas a certaine act of assembly held at James Citty the 8th day of June, in the yeare of our Lord 1780, intituled, an act prevent negroes insurrections hath not had its intended effect for want of due notice thereof being taken; Bee it enacted by the governour, councell and burgesses of this generall assembly, and by the authority thereof, that for the better putting the said act in due execution, the church wardens of each parish in this country at the

charge of the parish by the first day of January next provide true coppies of this present and the aforesaid act, and make or cause entry thereof to be made in the register book of the said parish, and that the minister or reader of each parish shall twice every yeare vizt. some one Sunday or Lords day in each of the months of September and march in each parish church or chappell of ease in each parish in the time of divine service, after the reading of the second lesson, read and publish both this present and the aforerecited act uner paine such churchwarden minister or reader makeing default, to forfeite each of them six hundred pounds of tobacco, one halfe to the informer and the other halfe to the use of the poore of the said parish. And for the further better preventing such insurrections by negroes or slaves, Bee it likewise enacted by the authority aforesaid, that noe master or overseer knowingly permitt or suffer, without the leave or licence of his or their master or overseer, any negroe or slave not properly belonging to him or them, to remaine or be upon his or their plantation above the space of four houres at any one time, contrary to the intent of the aforerecited act upon paine to forfeite, being thereof lawfully convicted, before some one justice of peace within the county where the fact shall be comitted, by the oath of two witnesses at the least, the summe of two hundred pounds of tobacco in cask for each time soe offending to him or them that will sue for the same, for which the said justice is hereby impowered to award judgment and execution.

April, 1691
Act XVI.
An act for suppressing outlying Slaves

Whereas many times negroes, mulattoes, and other slaves unlawfully absent themselves from their masters and mistresses service, and lie hid and lurk in obscure places killing hoggs and committing other injuries to the inhabitants of this dominion, for remedy whereof for the future, *Be it enacted by their majesties lieutenant governour, councell and burgesses of this present generall assembly, and the authoritie thereof, and it is hereby enacted,* that in all such cases upon intelligence of any such negroes, mulattoes or other slave lying out, two of their majesties justices of the peace of that county, whereof one to be of the quorum, where such negroes, mulattoes or other slave shall be shall be impowered and commanded, and are hereby impowered and commaned to issue out their warrants directed to the sherrife of the same county to apprehend such negroes, mulattoes, and other slaves, which said sherriffe is hereby likewise required upon all such occasions to raise such and soe many forces from time to time as he shall think convenient and necessary for the effectual apprehending such negroes, mulattoes and other slaves and in case any negroes, mulattoes or other slave or slaves lying out as aforesaid shall resist, runaway, or refuse to deliver and surrender him or themselves to any person or person that shall be by lawfull authority employed to apprehend and take such negroes, mulattoes or other slaves that in such cases it shall and may be lawfull for such person and persons to kill and distroy such negroes, mulattoes, and other slave or slaves by gunn or any otherwaise whatsoever.
Provided that where any negroe or mulattoe slave or slaves shall be killed in pursuance of this act, the owner or owners of such negro or mulatto slave shall be paid for such negro or mulattoe slave four thousand pounds of tobacco by the publique. And for prevention of that abominable and spurious issue which hereafter may encrease in this dominion, as well by negroes, mulattoes, and Indians intermarrying with English, or other white women, as by their unlawfull accompanying with one another, *Be it enacted by the authoritie aforesaid, and it is hereby enacted,* that for the time to come, whatsoever English or other white man or woman being free shall intermarry with a negroe, mulatto, or Indian man or woman bond or free shall within three months after such marriage be banished and removed from this dominion forever, and that the justices of each respective countie within this dominion make it their perticular care, that this act be put in effectuall execution. *And be it further enacted by the authoritie aforesaid, and it is hereby enacted,* That if any English woman being free shall have a bastard child by any negro or mulatto, she pay the sume of fifteen pounds sterling, within one moneth after such bastard child shall be born, to the Church wardens of the parish where she shall be delivered of such child, and in default of such payment she shall be taken into the possession of the said Church wardens and disposed of for five yeares, and the said fine of fifteen pounds, or whatever the woman shall be disposed of for, shall be paid, one third part to their majesties for and towards the support of the government and the contingent charges thereof, and one other third part to the use of the parish where the offence is committed, and the other third part to the informer, and that such bastard child be bound out as a servant by the said Church wardens untill he or she shall attaine the age of thirty yeares, and in case such English woman that shall have such bastard child be a servant, she shall be sold by the said church wardens, (after her time is expired that she ought by law to serve her master) for five yeares, and the money she shall be sold for divided as is before appointed, and the child to serve as aforesaid.
And forasmuch as great inconveniences may happen to this country by the setting of negroes and mulattoes free, by their either entertaining negro slaves from their masters service, or receiveing stolen goods, or being grown

old bringing a charge upon the country; for prevention thereof, *Be it enacted by the authority aforesaid, and it is hereby enacted, The no negro or mulattoe be after the end of the present session of assembly set free by any person or person whatsoever, unless such person or persons, their heires, executors or administrator pay for the transportation of such negro or negroes out of the countrey within six moneths after such setting them free, upon penalty of paying of tenn pounds sterling to the Church wardens of the parish where such person shall be necessary, the said Church wardens are to cause the said negro or mulatto to be transported out of the countrey, and the remainder of the said money to imploy to the use of the poor of the parish.*

1705
Chapter 49

IV, *And also be it Enacted,* by the Authority aforesaid, and it is hereby enacted, That all Servants imported and brought into this Country by Sea or Land, who were not Christians, in their native Country, (except Turks and Moors in Amity with Her Majesty, and Others that can make due Proof of their being Free in England, or any other Christian Country, before they were shipped, in order to Transportation hither) shall be accounted and be slaves, and as such be here brought and sold, notwithstanding a Conversion to Christianity afterwards.

V. *And be it Enacted,* by the Authority aforesaid, and it is hereby Enacted, That if any person or Persons shall hereafter import into this Colony, and heresell as a Slave, any Person or Persons that shall have been a Freeman in any Christian Country, Island, or Plantation, such Importer and Seller as aforesaid, shall forfeit and pay, to the party from whom the said Free shall recover his Freedom, double the Sum for which the said Freeman was sold; to be recovered, in any Court of Record within this Colony, according to the Court of the Common Law, wherein the Defendant shall not be admitted to plead in Bar, any Act or Statue for Limitation of Actions.

VI. *Provided always,* That a Slave's being in England, shall not be sufficient to discharge him of his Slavery, without other Proof of his being manumitted there.

Act XXII
English running away with negroes.

Bee itt enacted That in case any English servant shall run away in company with any negroes who are incapable of makeing satisfaction by addition of time, Bee itt enacted that the English so running away in company with them shall serve for the time of the said negroes absence as they are to do for the owne by a former act.

May 1782-6th of Commonwealth
Chapter. XXI
An act to authorize the manumission of slaves

I. Whereas application hath been made to this present general assembly, that those persons who are disposed to emancipate their slaves may be empowered so to do, and the same hath been judged expedient under certain restrictions: *Be it therefore enacted,* That it shall hereafter be lawful for any person, by his or her last will and testament, or by any other instrument in writing, under his or her hand and seal, attested and proved in the county court by two witnesses, or acknowledged by the party in the court of the county where he or she resides, to emancipate and set free, his or her slaves, or any other, who shall thereupon be entirely and fully discharged from the performance of any contract entered into during servitude, and enjoy as full freedom as if they had been particularly named and freed by this act.

I. *Provided always, and be it further enacted,* That all slaves so set free, not being in the judgment of the court, of sound mind and body, or being above the age of forty-five years, or being males under the age of twenty-one, or females under the age of eighteen years, shall respectively be supported and maintained by the person so liberating them, or by his or her estate; and upon neglect or refusal so to do, the court of the county where such neglect or refusal may be, is hereby empowered and required, upon application to them made, to order the sheriff to distrain and sell so much of the person's estate as shall be sufficient for the purpose. *Provided also,* That every person by written instrument in his life time, or if by last will and testament, the executors of every person freeing any slave, shall cause to be delivered to him or her, a copy of the instrument of emancipation, attested by the clerk of the court of the county, who shall be paid therefore, by the person emancipating, five shillings, to be collected in the manner of other clerk's fees. Every person neglecting or refusing to deliver any slave by him or her set free, such copy, shall forfeit and pay ten pounds, to be recovered with costs in any court of record, one half thereof to the person suing for the same, and the other to the person to whom such copy ought to have been delivered. it shall be lawful for any justice of the peace to commit to the gaol of his county, any emancipated slave travelling out of the county of his or her residence without a copy of the instrument of his or emancipation, there to remain till such copy is produced and gaoler's fee paid.

III. *And be it further enacted*, That in case any slave so liberated shall neglect in any year to pay all taxes levies imposed or to be imposed by law, the court of the county shall order the sheriff to hire our him or her for so long time as will raise the said taxes and levies. *Provided* sufficient distress cannot be made upon his or her estate. Saving *nevertheless* to all and every person and persons, bodies politic or corporate, and their heirs and successors, other than the person or persons claiming under those so emancipating their slaves, all such right and title as they or any of them could or might claim if this act had never been made.

1783
Chapter CXC
An Act directing the emancipation of certain Slaves who have served as Soldiers in this State and for the emancipation of the Slave Aberdeen.

Section 1. Whereas it hath been represented to the present General Assembly, that during the course of the way, many persons in this State had caused their slaves to enlist in certain regiments of corps raised with the same, having tendered such slaves to the Officers appointed to recruit forces within the State, as substitutions for free persons, whose lot or duty it was to serve in such regiments or corps, at the same time representing to such recruiting Officers that the slaves so enlisted by their direction and concurrence were freemen; and it appearing further to this Assembly, that on the expiration of the term of enlistment of such slaves that the former owners have attempted again to force them to return to a state of servitude, contrary to the principles of justice, and to their own solemn promise, AND WHEREAS it appears just and reasonable that all persons enlisted as aforesaid, who have faithfully served agreeable to the terms of their enlistment, and have thereby of course contributed towards the establishment of American liberty and independence, should enjoy the blessings of freedom as a reward for their toils and labours;

Section 2. *Be it therefore enacted*, That each and every slave, who by the appointment and direction of his owner, hath enlisted in any regiment or corps raised within this State, either a Continental or State establishment, and hath been received as a substitute for any free person whose duty or lot it was to serve in such regiment or corps, and hath served faithfully during the term of such enlistment, or hath been discharged from such service by some Officer duly authorised to grant such discharge, shall from and after the passing of this Act, be fully and compleatly emancipated, and shall be held and deemed from in as full and ample a manner as if each and every ____ were especially named in this Act; and the Attorney-General for the Commonwealth, is hereby required to commence and action, in forma pauperis, in behalf of any of the person____described who shall after the passing of this Act be detained in servitude by any person.

1810
Chapter XXX
Page 57

2. No free negro or mulatto shall be allowed to carry on board of his boat any gun, rifle or other fire arms, under pain or forfeiting the same to the use of any white person, who may seize them, any law to the contrary notwithstanding; nor shall any owner of any slave permit him to carry such arms, under the like forfeiture.

3. If any waterman of colour be found strolling from his boar above the banks of the river or any of its branches, while on a trip up or down, and not at his usual place of abode, or at any place while loading, it shall be lawful for any person or persons to carry him before the nearest magistrate, who may cause him to be whipped with any number of lashes not exceeding twenty: *Provided*, nothing herein contained shall be so construed as to prevent watermen from going directly to and from any spring for the purpose of getting water; *And provided always*, that when any waterman shall be ordered by any magistrate to receive any number of lashes, he may release himself therefrom, by paying to the said magistrate the sum of two dollars for the use of the poor of his county or corporation.

4. And if any waterman or watermen, being free, shall hereafter be detected in stealing or burning rails or other wood already cut, cuting locust or other trees, stealing grain of any kind, live stock of any kind, or other thing what ever, and be convicted thereof before any justice of the peace having jurisdiction of the case, shall forfeit and pay to the owner of the property so stolen, cut or burnt, treble the value thereof, to be fixed by the judgment of the justice before whom such offender may be convicted, upon such evidence as to him shall be convincing; which justice is justice is hereby required to issue execution, against the good and chattels of the offender, in favor of the owner of any such stolen property, for the amount of such judgment and costs of prosecution, directed to any sheriff or constable, who shall execute and return the same, and be liable to the same remedies and fines for neglect of duty in case of other executions. And the said offender or offenders shall suffer such other pains and neglect of duty in case of other executions. And the said offender or offenders shall suffer such other pains and punishments as are by law for such offences made and provided. But when the testimony of the owner of the property so stolen, cut or burnt, shall be necessary to the conviction of the offender or offenders, the same course shall be pursued, except that the forfeiture of three times the value shall be paid to the magistrate who issued the execution or executions, for the use of the poor of his county, or corporation; And when any slave or slaves shall be convicted of any or either of the aforesaid offences, the owner of or person hiring the said slave or slaves shall forfeit any pay to the owner of the property so stolen, cut or burnt, the full and equal value thereof to be ascertained and recovered against such owner of, or person hiring as in the case of a free person, and the said slave or slaves shall receive twenty lashes on his or their bare backs for the first offence, and for the second offence, the same forfeiture shall be incurred by such master or person hiring and double the number of lashes inflicted upon such offender, and for the third offence, as well as for every

1831
Chapter XXII
An Act to amend an act entitled "an act reducing into one the several acts concerning slaves, free negroes and mulattoes and ____ other purposes."

1. Be it enacted by the general assembly, That no slave free negro or mulatto, whether he shall have been ordained or licensed, or otherwise, shall hereafter undertake to preach, exhort or conduct or hold any assembly or meeting, for religious or other purposes either in the day time, or at night; and any slave, free negro or mulatto, so offending, shall for every such offence, be punished with stripes, at the discretion of any justice of the peace, not exceeding thirty-nine lashes; and any person desiring so to do, shall have authority, without say previous written precept or otherwise to apprehend any such justice.

2. Any slave, free negro or mulatto, who shall hereafter attend any preaching, meeting or other assembly, held or pretended to be held for religious purposes, or other instruction, conducted by any slave, free negro or mulatto preacher, ordained or otherwise; and any slave who shall hereafter attend any preaching in the night time, although conducted by a white minister, without a written permission from his or her owner, overseer or master or agent of either of them, shall be punished by stripes at the discretion of any justice of the peace, not exceeding thirty-nine lashes; and may for that purpose be apprehended by any person, without any written or other precept; Provided, that nothing herein contained shall be so construed, as to prevent the masters or owners of slave, or any white person to whom any free negro or mulatto is bound, or in whose employment, or on whose plantation or let such free negro or mulatto, to go with him, her or them, or with any part of his, her, or their white family to any place of religious worship, conducted by a white minister, in the night time; And provided also, That nothing in this or any former law, shall be so construed, as to prevent any ordained or licensed white minister of the gospel or any layman licensed for that purpose by the denomination to which he may belong, from preaching, or giving religious instruction to slaves, free negroes and mulattoes, in the day time; not to deprive any master or owners of slaves of the right to engage, or employ any free white person whom they may think proper, to give religious instruction to their slaves; nor to prevent the assembling of the slave of any one owner or master together, at any time for religious devotion.

3. No free negroe or mulatto shall hereafter be capable of purchasing or otherwise acquiring permanent ownership, except by descent, to any slave, other than his or her husband, wife or children; and all contracts for any such purchase are hereby declared to be null and void.

4. No free negro or mulatto shall be suffered to keep or carry any firelock of any kind, any military weapon, or any powder or lead; and any free negro or mulatto who shall so offend, shall, on conviction to the use of the informer; and shall moreover be punished with stripes, at the discretion of the justice, not exceeding thirty-nine lashes. And the provise to the seventh section of the act, entitled, "an act reducing into one the several acts concerning slave, free negroes and mulattoes" passed the second day of march, one thousand eight hundred and nineteen, authorising justices of the peace, in certain cases to permit slaves to keep and use guns or other

weapons, powder and shot; and so much of the eighth section of the said recited act as authorised the county and corporation and courts to grant licenses to free negroes and mulattoes to keep or carry any firelock of any kind, any military weapon, or any powder or lead, shall be the same and the same are hereby repealed.

5. No slave, free negro or mulatto shall hereafter be permitted to sell, give, or otherwise dispose of any ardent or spiritous liquor at or within one mile of any master, preaching, or other public assembly of black or white person; and any slave, free negro or mulatto, so offending, shall be punished by stripes, at the discretion of a justice of the peace, not exceeding thirty-nine.

6. If any slave free negro or mulatto, shall hereafter wilfully and maliciously assault and beat any white person, with intention in so doing kill such white person; every such slave, free negro or mulatto, so offending, and being thereof lawfully convicted, shall be adjudged and deemed guilty of felony, and shall suffer death without benefit of clergy.

7. If any person shall hereafter write, print, or cause to be written or printed, any book, pamphlet or other writing, advising persons of colour within this state to make insurrection, or to rebel, or shall knowingly circulate, or cause to be circulated, any book, pamphlet or other writing, written or printed, advising persons of colour in this commonwealth to commit insurrection or rebellion; such person, if slave or free negro or mulatto, shall, on conviction before any justice of the peace, be punished for the first offence with stripes at the discretion of the said justice, not exceeding thirty-nine lashes; and for the second offence, shall be deemed guilty of felony, and on due conviction, shall be punished, with death with benefit of clergy; and if the person so offending be a white person, he or she shall be punished on conviction, in a sum of not less than one hundred nor more than one thousand dollars.

8. Riots, routs, unlawful assemblies, trespasses and sedition speeches, by free negroes or mulattoes, shall hereafter be punished with stripes, in the same mode, and to the same extent, as slaves are directed to punished by the twelfth section of the before recited act.

9. If any free negro or mulatto shall hereafter commit simple larceny of any money, bank note, good, chattels, or other thing of value of twenty dollars or less, he or she, for such offences, shall be tried and punished in the same manner as slaves are directed to be tried and punished by the fifth section of the act, entitled "an act concerning the trial and punishment of slaves, free negroes and mulattoes in certain cases, "passed the twelfth day of February, one thousand eight hundred and twenty-eight.

10. If any white person, free negro or mulatto, shall hereafter receive from any slave, free negro or mulatto, any stolen goods, knowing the said goods to have been stolen, he or she shall be adjudged guilty or larceny of the said goods, and punished in the same manner, and to the same extent, as if the receiver had actually stolen the said goods; but nothing herein contained shall be so construed as to prevent to prosecution, conviction and punishment of the person who actually shall have stolen them, as heretofore.

11. Free negroes and mulattoes shall hereafter be presented, tried, convicted, and punished for any felony, by justices of oyer and terminer, in the same manner as slaves are not prosecuted, tried, convicted and punished; and any court summoned or adjourned for such trial, shall have and exercise all the powers and incidents of a court summoned or adjourned for the trial of a slave except that in cases of homicide, and in cases where the punishment shall be death, the mode of trial shall remain as heretofore.

12. Nothing in this act contained shall be so construed as to bar or conclude any prosecution for any offence committed previously to this act going into operation, but the same shall be so conducted, decided and executed, as if this act had never passed.

13. It shall be the duty of the several judges of this commonwealth, and presiding justices of the county and corporation courts, constantly to give this act in charge to the grand juries; and it is moreover made the duty of all attornies prosecuting for the commonwealth in any court therein, who may know of, or have good reason to suspect any violation of this act, to lodge information thereof before the proper court or grand jury, and to institute forthwith the proper prosecution for his or her conviction.

14. This act shall commence and be in force from and after the first day of July next.

Chapter XXIII
Page 23
An act concerning the county of Northampton

Whereas from a representation made to this general assembly by the people of Northampton county, it satisfactorily appears that it is absolutely necessary, not only to the correct government of their slaves, but also to the peace and safety of their society, that the free people of colour should be promptly removed from that county; and also, in order to effect their removal in a manner as humane and as little as oppressive as possible, the people of the said county, assembled in public meetings, have appointed a committee with authority to borrow a sum of many not exceeding fifteen thousand dollars, to be reimbursed by an annual tax to be levied on the people thereof. And whereas the said people have petitioned this present general assembly for the passage of such laws as may be necessary to carry into effect, the purposes and resolution of said meetings so far as the same may form proper subjects of public legislation:

1. Be it therefore enacted, That the proceedings of the said public meetings and the acts done, or to be done by the said committee, in pursuance of the authority vested in them as aforesaid, shall be and the same are hereby charged as a debt upon the said county of Northampton.

2. And be it further enacted, That all such sums of money as the said committee have borrowed or may hereafter borrow, by virtue of the authority aforesaid, not exceeding fifteen thousand dollars, shall be, and the same are hereby charged as a debt upon the said county of Northampton.

3. And be it further enacted, That the county court of the said county shall at the time at which the said court shall lay the county levy, direct the sheriff of the said county, at the time that he collects the revenue tax, received from each and every person liable to pay the said revenue tax, a sum, to be designated by said court.

4. And be it further enacted, That in collecting the said sums for the purpose aforesaid the sheriff shall possess the same rights, authority and powers, and shall proceed in all respects, in the manner, which is or shall be directed by law, for the collection of the revenue tax, and shall be subject to the same penalties and forfeitures for refusing or failing to collect or pay the same as are or shall be imposed by law for neglecting or refusing to collect or pay parish and county levy, to be moved and recovered in the same manner; provided, That no higher commission than five per centum shall be allowed for collecting and paying and said money.

5. This act shall commence and be in force from and after its passage.

December, 1831

2. *Be it further enacted*, That if any master or skipper of any steam-boat or other vessel, or any other person shall bring in to this commonwealth, by water or by land, in any steam-boat or other vessel, boat, land, carriage or otherwise, any free negro or mulatto, such master or skipper, if a white person, shall be deemed guilty of a high misdemeanor, and on conviction thereof before any circuit superior court of law and chancery, or any county or corporation court of this commonwealth, shall be punished by imprisonment in the common jail of this county or corporation wherein such conviction shall be had, for a term not less than six months, nor more than twelve months, and by a fine not less than five hundred, nor more than one thousand dollars, at the direction of the court. And if any master, skipper, or other person offending as aforesaid, shall be a free negro or mulatto, such offender shall, on conviction thereof before any justice of the peace, receive not less than twenty, nor more than thirty-nine lashes, on his or her bare back, at the public whipping post. It shall be the duty of all sheriffs, sergeant and constables to use their best endeavors to enforce the provisions of this section; and in case the same be violated by any white person, to give information and make complaint thereof on oath to some justice of the peace, who shall thereupon issue his warrant to cause the party to be arrested and brought before him, or some other justice of his county or corporation; and if on examination, there appear to be reasonable ground for believing that such party is guilty, the justice shall commit him or her to the jail of the said county or corporation, to answer a bill of indictment for the said offences, to be preferred at the next quarterly term of the court of such county or corporation, unless the person charged with the said offence shall enter into recognizance in the sum of one thousand dollars with two sufficient sureties, in the sum of five hundred dollars each, conditioned that the accused shall appear at such quarterly term to answer the said indictment; and, in either case, the examining justice shall take the recognizances of all material witnesses against the accused, with condition to appear at the same term to give evidence on behalf of the commonwealth upon such indictment.

3. Be it further enacted, That this act shall not extend to say person traveling into and through this commonwealth, who shall have any free negro or mulatto bona fide in his or her employment as a servant, not to any master or skipper of a steam-boat or other vessel bringing into this commonwealth any free negro or mulatto bona fide employed on board such steam-boat or other vessel or belonging thereto, and who shall therewith depart: Provided, That it any such free negro or mulatto, as in this section mentioned, shall be found away from the steam-boat or other vessel to which he or she belongs, or from the lodgings of his or her master or employer except on the express business of such master or employer, unless he or she shall have a written permission from the skipper of any such steam-boat or other vessel, or from the employer of such free negro or mulatto, (the burthen of the proof whereof shall be upon such free negro or mulatto,) it shall be lawful for any citizen, and it shall be the duty of all sheriffs, sergeants, and constables, to apprehend such free negro or mulatto, and convey him or her before any justice of the peace of the county or corporation wherein such arrest may be made; and if, on

examination, it shall appear that any such free negro or mulatto is guilty of the offence in this section declared, he or she shall receive not less than twenty nor more than thirty-nine lashes on his or her bare back, and thereafter be delivered to his or her master or employer.

4. *Be it farther enacted,* That if any master or skipper of a steam-boat or other vessel, shall knowingly receive on board the same any runaway slave, and permit his or her to remain on board, such master or skipper shall be deemed guilty of felony; and if a free person, shall, on conviction, be imprisoned in the public jail or penitentiary house for a period of not less than two, nor more than five years; and if a slave, shall receive * lashes on his bare back, at the public whipping post: *Provided,* That if any slave be found on board of any steam-boat or other vessel after leaving port, the master or skipper thereof shall be presumed to have knowingly received such slave on board.

5. *Be it farther enacted,* That it shall be lawful for any justice of the peace, when he shall be satisfied by affidavit or otherwise, that any runaway slave or slaves is or are on board any steam-boat or other vessel within the waters over which the jurisdiction of this commonwealth extends, to issue his warrant, commanding any officer or other person whom he may appoint to execute the same to search the said steam-boat or other vessel, and to bring before him, or some other justice of his county or corporation, any runaway slave or slaves who may be found on board; whereupon, such slave or slaves shall be dealt with as the law directs; and the said warrant shall also command the officer or other person charged with execution thereof, in case any runaway slave be found on board, to apprehend the master or skipper of such steam-boat or other vessel, and bring him before the justice issuing the warrant, or some other justice of the same county or corporation; whereupon, the like proceedings shall be had against such master or skipper, as are directed in other cases of felony.

6. *Be it farther enacted,* That if any free person shall entice, advise or persuade any slave to abscond fro his or her owner or possessor, or shall procure, furnish or deliver to, or for any slave any register, pass, or other writing whatsoever, or any money, clothes or provisions, with intent in so doing to aid such slave to abscond from his or her owner or possessor, every such person of offending, and his or her aiders and abettors, being free, shall be deemed guilty of felony, and on conviction, shall be sentenced to imprisonment in the public jail and penitentiary house for a period not less than two nor more than five years. If a slave shall commit, aid or abet any such offence as in this section is aforesaid, he or she, on conviction thereof before a justice of the peace, shall receive thirty-nine lashes on his or her bare back; if after such conviction, such slave shall at any time be guilty of a second offence against this section, he or she shall be deemed a felon, within the benefit of clergy, and on conviction, shall be punished accordingly; and if after such conviction for felony, such slave at any time be guilty of a third offence against this section, he or she shall be deemed a felon, and on conviction, receive thirty-nine lashes on his or her bare back, and be transported and banished beyond the limits of the United States.

7. *Be it farther enacted,* That if any free person shall hereafter commit any of the offences mentioned in the seventh section of the act passed the fifteenth day of march, eighteen hundred and thirty-two, entitled, "an act to amend an act, entitled 'an act reducing into one the several acts concerning slaves, free negroes and mulattoes, and for other purposes.'" such person shall be deemed guilty of felony, and on due conviction, shall be imprisoned in the public jail and penitentiary house for a period not less than two not more than five years.

8. Be it enacted, That any prosecution of behalf of the commonwealth against any offender or offenders against the provisions of the thirtieth and thirty-first sections of the act passed the second of March, eighteen hundred and nineteen, entitled, "an act reducing into one the several acts concerning slaves, free negroes and mulattoes," or any action authorized by said act for the recovery of double the value of any slave or slaves, with costs and expenses, may be tried either in the county from which the said slave or slaves shall be taken or removed, or in any other county of this commonwealth, wherein the defendant or defendants shall have given countenance, protection or assistance to such slave or slaves, for the purpose of preventing him, her or them from being stopped or apprehended, or otherwise aided him, her, or them in escaping beyond the limits of the commonwealth.

9. *And be it farther enacted,* That if any person or persons shall have offended against the provisions of the above recited act, and thereby given to another right of action or suit for the recovery of double the value of any slave or slaves, together with double the amount of all costs and expenses incurred in regaining or attempting to regain such slave or slaves, and such offender or offenders shall ha have departed this commonwealth, leaving property real or personal, or debts due or to become due to him or them therein, it shall be lawful for the owner or owners of the slave or slaves so lost to file his bill in chancery in the circuit superior court of law and chancery of the county from which the slave or slaves shall have been removed, or in any other county of this commonwealth been removed or in any other county of this commonwealth through which they may have passed in leaving the same, making the said offender or offenders, together with all persons indebted to him or them, or having in possession goods or effects, lands or tenements belong to him or them, defendants to his bill, and stating therein what lands know to the plaintiff, the defendant or defendants may own in the commonwealth,

and thereupon the clerk of the said court shall issue a subpoena and endorse the same as in other cases of proceeding against absent defendants, a and the proceedings in such suit shall be similar to those common in such cases. And the court before whom any such suit shall be depending, shall cause an issue to be made up on the allegations contained in said bill: and if the jury shall find the facts for the complainant, they shall assess the damages by him sustained, and the court shall render a decree for double the amount of the damages so assessed, and for costs.

10. *Be it farther enacted,* That it shall not be lawful for the clerk of any corporation court to register any free negro or mulatto unless by the order of such court. In addition to the particulars of description now required by law, such register shall specify any apparent mark or scar on the face, hear or hands of such free negro or mulatto; and by what instrument, whether deed or will, such negro or mulatto was emancipated, and the deed of the record thereof; and upon every renewal of any such register, it shall be the duty of the clerk so to modify and alter the original register as to identify the individual to whom it is given; for which renewal, the clerk shall be entitled to demand and receive the sum of fifty cents

11. All acts and parts of acts within the purview of this act shalbe, and the same are hereby repealed: *Provided, nevertheless,* That offences committed before the passing of this act, may and shall be prosecuted, tried and punished as if this act had never been passed.

12. This act shall be in force from the passing thereof.

1832
CHAPTER 12
Page 14
An Act to appropriate for the removal of free persons of colour.

1. *Be it enacted* by the general assembly, That the sum of eighteen thousand dollars shall be, and the same is hereby appropriated, to be paid annually, for the period of five years, out of any money in the treasury, not otherwise appropriated, for that purpose, and in the means herein after prescribed.

2. *Be it further enacted,* That the governor, lieutenant governor, first and second auditors, for the time being, shall be and they are hereby constituted a board of commissioners, for the purpose of carrying into effect the provision of this act, any two of whom shall be a quorum for said purpose.

3. Whenever satisfactory proof shall be produced to the said board of commissions, that any number of free persons of colour, shall have been actually transported to the colony at Liberia, or other place on the western coast of Africa, or that they shall have been embarked for transportation thither, from within the limits of this commonwealth, by the American colonization society, it shall be lawful, and the said board of commissioners are hereby required to issue their warrant on the treasury of this commonwealth, for such sum or sums of money as may be necessary to defray the costs of transporting and subsisting such free persons of colour for a limited time, on the said coast of Africa, payable to the authorized and accredited agent or agents of the said American colonization society: *Provided,* that the sum or sums which may, from time to time, be thus expended, shall, in no one year, exceed the amount hereby appropriated for such year, and that the free persons of colour who may be removed, under the provisions of this act, shall be selected from the different counties and corporations of this commonwealth, in proportion to the amount of revenue paid into the public treasury by such county or corporation, if such free persons of colour can be found in such county or corporation, willing to emigrate, but if the whole sum of money hereby appropriated to each county and corporation shall not be annually applied to the removal of such free persons of colour therein, because of their unwillingness to emigrate therefrom, then the balance thereof may be equitably applied, by the said board of commissioners, to the removal of free persons of colour from other counties and corporations: *And provided further,* That not more than the sum of thirty dollars, shall be allowed by said board of commissioners for the transportation and subsistence as aforesaid, of any free person of colour, above the age of ten years, and not more than the sum of twenty dollars, for the transportation and subsistence of any free person of colour, under the said age of ten years. And the said board of commissioner are hereby required to keeps and exact account of all monies disbursed under the authority of this act, and to make an annual report thereof to the general assembly, shewing the ages and sex of such free persons of colour as may be transported from the commonwealth, and the counties, cities or boroughs from which they may have been respectively removed; together with such other facts or suggestions as they may deem interesting or proper: *Provided,* That no payment shall be made by the same board under the provisions of this act, for the transportation of any other than persons of colour who are now free, and born and residing within the commonwealth of their descendants.

4. This act shall be enforce from and after the passage thereof.

December, 1836
Chapter 7
An Act amending the laws concerning emancipated slaves, free negroes and mulattoes Passed March 22, 1837

Whereas many petitions are annually presented to the general assembly from emancipated slaves, praying permission to remain within the commonwealth, and it being the desire of the legislature to fee itself from such subjects of legislation, and to refer the same to some more appropriate tribunal, where the merits of such petitions may be more fully considered:

1. *Be it there enacted* by the general assembly, That any slave who hath been emancipated since the first day of May, eighteen hundred and six, or who may hereafter be emancipated, shall be at liberty to apply to the court of any county or corporation for permission to reside within such county or corporation; and the court to which such application shall be made, the acting justices thereof having been first summoned, and a majority of them being actually present, shall have power, upon satisfactory proof made to them that the applicant is a person of good character, peaceable, orderly and industrious, and not addicted to drunkenness, gaming, or any other vice, to grant to him or her permission to remain within the commonwealth, and to reside within such county or corporation only, during the good pleasure of the court; *Provided however*, That no such permission shall be granted unless notice of the application shall have been posted at the front door of the courthouse of the county or corporation for at least two months immediately preceding such application, nor unless three fourths of the justices present shall concur, not unless the attorney for the commonwealth, or in his absence some other attorney to be appointed by the court for the purpose, shall appear on behalf of the commonwealth and defend such application; *And provided also*, That no such permission shall be granted, or shall be valid if granted, unless the court shall enter of record that the person to whom it is granted is of the character and discription herein before required, and the attorney for the commonwealth or some other attorney appointed for the purpose as aforesaid was preseng and represented the interests of the commonwealth in the case; *And provided*, That the provisions of this act shall not extend to those persons heretofore emancipated, who are not now residents of this commonwealth.

2. *And be it further enacted*, That the several county and corporation courts of this commonwealth, the acting justices thereof having been first summoned, and a majority being present, shall have power and authority, for any cause deemed sufficient by them, to revoke any permission of residence so as aforesaid granted to any emancipated person, having first had him or her duly summoned to shew cause against it. If after such revocation any such person shall remain within this commonwealth more than twelve months, he, she or they so remaining , shall forfeit their right to freedom, and may be apprehended and sold in the manner prescribed by law in relation to slaves emancipated and remaining in the state more than one year.

3. *And be it further enacted*, That all persons obtaining permission of residence under the provisions of this act, who may leave the commonwealth and thereafter return into the same, may be apprehended and dealt with in the same manner as is provided by law, in relation to free negroes and mulattoes migrating into this commonwealth; *Provided however*, That no such free negro or mulatto, or slave emancipated as aforesaid, shall be sujected to the penalties imposed by this act for merely passing through the state.

4. *And be it further enacted*, That nothing in this or any other act contained shall be so construed as to authorize the sheriff or other officer to charge or receive any fee or regard for summoning the justices of his county or corporation under the provisions of this act.

5. *And be it further enacted*, That all acts and parts of acts coming within the purview of this act, shall be, and the same are hereby repealed.

6. *Be it further enacted*, That in consequence of the peculiar position of the counties of Accomack and Northampton, the said counties be and they are hereby exempted from the operation of the provisions of this act.

7. This act shall be in force from the passing thereof.

January, 1838
Chapter 99
An Act to prevent free persons of colour who leave the state from returning to it in certain cases.

1. *Be it enacted by the general assembly*, That if any free person of colour, whether infant or adult, shall go or be sent or carried beyond the limits of this commonwealth for the purpose of being educated, he or she shall be deemed to have emigrated from the state, and it shall not be lawful for him or her to return to the same; and

if any such person shall return within the limits of the state contrary to the provisions of this act, he or she being an infant, shall be bound out as an apprentice until the age of twenty-one years, by the overseers of the poor of the county or corporation where he or she may be, and at the expiration of that period, shall be sent of the state agreeably to the provisions of the laws now in force, or which may hereafter be enacted to prohibit the migration of free persons of colour to this state; and if such person be an adult, he or she shall be sent in like manner out of the commonwealth; and if any person having been so sent off, shall thereafter return within the state, he or she of offending shall be dealt with and punished in the same manner as is or may be prescribed by law in relation to other persons of colour returning to the state after having been sent therefrom.

2. This act shall be in force from and after the first day of August next.

January, 1839
Chapter 31
An Act concerning patrols

1. *Be it enacted by the general assembly of Virginia*, That patrols are hereby authorized to force open the doors of free negroes and mulattoes, and of slaves in the absence of their masters or overseers, when access denied, when in search of fire arms or other weapons, by authority of a warrant from a justice of the peace, issued for that purpose.

2. This act shall commence and be in force from and after the passing thereof.

December, 1842
Chapter 86
An Act to prevent free negroes and mulattoes in the county of Accomack and county of Richmond from selling agricultural products without a certificate.

1. *Be it enacted by the general assembly*, That hereafter it shall not be lawful for any free negro or mulatto in the county of Accomack and county of Richmond to sell or barter, or to offer to sell or barter, any indian corn, wheat, oats, peas, beans or other agricultural products, unless such free negro or mulatto shall first obtain the certificate in writing of two respectable white persons of the county or neighbourhood, stating their belief that he or she cultivated and raised the same, or came otherwise honestly by it. And any free negro or mulatto who shall forfeit the corn, wheat, oats, peas, beans or other products in his, her, or their possession at the time, to be sold by direction of the justice of the peace, and the proceeds thereof after deducting ten per cent as a compensation to the constable of other officer, for his services in that behalf, to be paid over by the said constable or other officer, for his services in that behalf, to be paid over by the said constable or other officer, to the overseers of the poor of the county for the benefit of the poor; and said free negro or mulatto shall moreover be punished with stripes at the discretion of the justice, not exceeding fifteen lashes.

2. *And be it further enacted*, That if any white person shall knowingly or wilfully purchase, or receive in trade, of any such free negro or mulatto, any corn, wheat, oats, peas, beans or other agricultural products, without the production of the certificate aforesaid, he, she, or they shall be deemed guilty of a misdemeanour: Provided, however, That noting in this act contained shall be construed to alter or affect in any manner, any law at present existing in relation to larceny, or the receivers of stolen goods, or to prevent prosecutions and punishments thereof.

3. This act shall be in force from the passing thereof.

December, 1843
Chapter 75
An Act to extend the provisions of "an act to prevent free negroes and mulattoes in the counties of Accomack and Richmond from selling agricultural products without a certificate, passed March 27th, 1843."

1. *Be it enacted by the general assembly*, That the provisions of an act, entitled "an act to prevent free negroes and mulattoes in the county of Accomack and county of Richmond from selling agricultural products with a certificate," passed march the twenty-seventh, eighteen hundred and forty-three, be and the same are hereby extended to the remaining counties and corporations of the commonwealth: *Provided* however, That before this act shall have any force in any county or corporation of the commonwealth, the court of such county or corporation, the acting justices thereof being summoned, and a majority thereof being present, shall approve thereof.

2. This act shall be in force from and after the passing thereof.

December, 1861
Chapter 26
An Act for the Voluntary Enslavement of Free Negroes, without compensation to the Commonwealth
Passed March 28, 1861

1. Be it enacted by the general assembly, that it shall be lawful for free persons of color, or persons of color who have heretofore or may hereafter be manumitted, to appear before the circuit court of any county or corporation in which such free persons of color or manumitted slaves may have resided for twelve months, and make application thereto to select a master of mistress, and become slaves.

2. Upon the application of such free persons of color or manumitted slaves before the circuit court of said county or corporation, and the person they wish to choose as master or mistress, the court shall proceed to examine each party separately, as well as such other persons as said court may see fit. At any examination, the attorney for the commonwealth shall be present and see that such examination is properly conducted, and that no injustice is done to the applicant.

APPENDIX III

NOTES ON THE WILLS

All wills of emancipation are transcribed as each appears in the will books in Northampton County Clerk's office. All of the wills were written after the passage of the 1782 act entitled "An act to authorise the manumission of slaves. There have been no spelling, capitalization or punctuation corrections made. There are many examples of spellings that are inconsistent with today's spelling. The use of the "s" in authorise rather than the "z" is one such example.

The will written by Betsey Gleeson was obviously written by a person other than herself. As can be seen she could not write as is evidenced by her signing her will with an X. This was also true of Luke Martin, her witness. There are several other wills with the X used as a signature.

It is interesting to note that in some instances the freed slave took the name of the slave-holder. In other cases the freed slave took a name completely different. Research in the area of slaves names has indicated that many slaves took the name of the slaveholder that was closest to the time a African was brought her from Africa. This would mean that the freed slave would take the name of the first slaveholder and keep it.

Please note that in the will of John Stokely, the Register spells his name Stockly and even Mr. Stokely spells it Stockely in the third paragraph of the will. Also the mother of Michael is only referred to as Anna. I have no record as to what her name is or why she was not referred to by a last name.

The will of John Upshur is being presented because one of the Free Negroes registered names the John Upshur will as the instrument of emancipation. The John Upshur will itself does not name any slave to be emancipated. In fact this particular will is very ambiguous as to what is to be done with the slaves.

WILLS OF EMANCIPATION

THE WILL OF JOHN UPSHUR EMANCIPATING NELSON CHURCH

In The name of God Amen. I John Upshur Sen: being weak in body, but of perfect mind and memory and understanding, so make and ordain this writing to be my last will and Testament in the manner following, to wit, My will is that all my just debts be paid and in case my personal estate shall not be sufficient to satisfy them, that my Executor hereafter named shall have full power and authority to sell any part of the whole of my real estate for the payment thereof. and my meaning is that my Negroes are not to compose any part of my personal estate for the payment of my said debts.

Item. I give and devise to my Son James: Upshur one fifth part of all my real & personal Estate during his may said son's natural life, remainder to my son in Law Edmund Bayly and his heirs in Trust and for the use, of the first, and every child of my said son James, who shall survive him,
and their Heirs; and in case there should be no child, or children of my son James descendants from any one or more of them living, at the time of my son James' Death, then remainder to the heirs general of all my other Children equally to be divided among them:

Item. All the rest of my estate real and personal I bequeath to be equally divided among my other four children, to wit, Elizabeth Dennis, Rachel Bayly, William M. Upshur and Sarah D. Upshur and their heirs forever.

Item. I appoint Littleton Dennis guardian to my Daughter Sarah Upshur D. Upshur and my son in Law Edmund Bayly Executor to this will. In Testimony whereof I have hereunto set my hand and Seal the 29th day of April in the year of our Lord Seventeen hundred and ninety nine-

                                                                      John Upshur Sen: (SEAL)

Signed, Sealed and pronounces
as the last will & Testament
in the presence of---------
Joseph Gale, Daniel Wallis, John Robins

At a Court held for Northampton County the 9th Day of December 1799
This will was proved by the Oaths of Joseph Gale and John Robins witnesses thereto, and ordered to be recorded: and on the motion of Littleton Upshur one of the Executors therein appointed, and he having taken the oath and entered into bond with Security according to law, certificate in granted him to obtain thereof in due forms.

                                                                Teste
                                                                Ex.-Thomas Lytt Savage CNC

WILL OF BETSEY GLEESON EMANCIPATING SARAH GLEESON AND HER MINOR SON PETER GLEESON.

In the Name of God Amen, I Betsey Gleeson of Northampton County do make and ordain this instrument of writing to be my last will and testament, to wit, Item I give unto my two negroes Sarah & Peter their full freedom and Liberty and this my will to be their emancipation and further leave my Boy Peter unto his Mother Sarah until he shall arrive to the age of Twenty one Years. Lastly I appoint my Friend Richards Dunton Jr. my Executor revoking any Will hereto fore made by Me In Testimony whereof have hereunto set my hand & Seal this second day of December 1805.

                      her
           Betsey X Gleeson (SEAL)
                    mark

Signed Sealed & published   his
in the presence of }   Luke X Martin
                              mark

At a Court for Northampton county the 13th: January 1806-
This Will was proved by the oath of Luke Martin Witness hereto, And ordered to be recorded.

Teste
Ex. Tho Lytt: Savage CNC

JOHN STOCKLY'S WILL EMANCIPATING MICHAEL ROAN AND HIS MOTHER, ANNA

I, John Stokely Sen. of Northampton County and State of Virginia, do hereby make my last will and testament in manner and form following, that is to say:

First: I direct my executors herein after to be named, or the survivor, or survivors of them, to sell all of my real estate at such time, as they or the cursor, or survivors of them, shall deem most available and advantageous: And all of my personal estate (negroes excepted as soon after my death, if that happens between the first day of October and the first day of March, as may be deemed expedient; but if I die between the first day of March and thirtieth of September, then it is my will and desire that the family and every thing belonging is the family be kept together for the purpose of making and saving the crop then pitched or to be pitched on the farm, and out of the proceeds of the latter, (personal estate) if sufficient to pay all of my just debts and funeral expenses; but if insufficient, then the residue of Said debts and funeral expenses to be paid out of the sale of my real estate.

Secondly: I give to my beloved wife, Rachel Stockely, and her heirs forever, in lieu of dower in my estate, (both real and personal) Seven hundred dollars ($700:00) to be paid to her by my executors. And also, give her all of the household furniture to got by her, and when we were married.

Thirdly, When my negro boy Michael Roan, arrives at the age of twenty-four years (which will be on the first day of March eighteen hundred and fifty-five (1855) I set him free and his mother Anna, also,-both to be hired out until the aforesaid first day of March 1855, the former for the for the benefit of my estate and the latter (with a right always of choosing her home) for the purpose of raising a fund, which will enable her to leave the state after the 1st day of March 1855. It is my will and desire, that my executors or the survivor or survivors of them loan annually the hires of said negro Anna, so that the fund may accumulate untill the aforesaid 1st day of March 1855 and then collect the same and pay it over to said negro woman Anna. I give to my negro boy Michael Roan, fifty dollars ($50) to be paid to him by my executors on the first day of March 1855, to enable him to leave the state within the a time allowed by law. But if said negroes Michael Roan and his mother Anna, or either of them, shall fail to avail themselves, himself or herself of their freedom, freely given by me by leaving the state within the time allowed by law (being repeatedly warned to do so, by my executor, and they are earnestly desired to warn them) then it is my will that said negroes Michael and his mother Anna, revert to my Estate and be divided among my residuary legatees herein after to be named in proportion to their several bequests.

Fourthly: I give to each of my sister's (Patsy Phillips) children now resident in Accomack County one hun- dred dollars, and also to my brother's (Jeremiah Stockly) children now resident in Accomack County one hundred dollars each, except Sylvester Stockly: and in lieu of him, I give his children, one hundred dollars to be equally divided among them.

Fifthly: I give to the children of my niece Margaret Mehollomes that may be living at my death, one hundred and fifty ($150) dollars each. I give the children of my nephew John Stockly, that may be living at my death one hundred dollars ($100) each. I give to my niece Sarah Floyd, two hundred dollars ($200) and I give to my nephew Charles Stockly, one hundred & fifty dollars ($100)

Sixthly: I give my deceased wife's nephew, Peter Scott, one hundred & fifty dollars ($150) conditioned; that he claims nothing from my estate for the sum due him from his father's estate; who died in Suffolk and I received say fifty dollars. I give to my deceased wife's niece Margaret Scott, one hundred dollars-conditioned; as before states, in her brother Peter's legacy.

Seventhly: My desire is to be buried along side of my deceased wife, Margaret, on the Warren land near Frank-town; and that the railing of the grave yard may be enlarged, so as to contain my said deceased wife, myself and our three children; and also, that my executors purchase for the head and foot of each of our graves.-head and foot stones (to wit: ten pieces, to mark distinctly our resting place and have them put up at the expense of my estate.

Eighthly: My desire is, that the residue of my estate, both real, personal & mixed, may be divided among the foregoing legatees, viz: Patsy Phillips' children; Jeremiah Stockly's children; Sarah Floyd, Charles Stockly; Peter Scott and Margaret Scott, in proportion to their several bequest. But if the whole of my estate should be insufficient to pay and satisfy the foregoing provisions and legacies, then and in that case, each of the legatees named as above in this clause of my will to loose in proportion to their several bequests.

And lastly: I do here by constitute and appoint my friends, Henry P. C. Wilson, Charles I. D.m, Wise and Jackson B. Powell executors of this my last will and testament, hereby revoking all other or former wills or testaments by me heretofore made.

In witness whereof, I have hereunto set my hand and affixed my Seal this day of July A. D. 1846.

John Stockly (SEAL)

Signed, Sealed, published and
declared, by John Stockly as and
for his last will and testament,
in the presence and hearing of us,
who, at his request and in his presence have subscribed our names as witnesses,
Smith Nottingham
Geo. T. Yerby - Tho. H. Bagwell

At a Court held for Northampton County the 9th day of August 1847.
This last Will and Testament of John Stockly___ was proved by the oaths of Smith Nottingham & George Yerby, two of the subscribing witnesses thereto & and ordered to be recorded.

Ex.   Teste. Louis P. Rogers C.N.C

The Will of Arthur Savage Emancipating Amy Savage, Lewis Fisher and David Heath.

I Arthur R. Savage of the County of Northampton and State of Virginia do make this my last Will and Testament as Follows, To Wit.

Item I give to my grandson Thomas Jacob Savage the sum of Three Thousand Dollars to be paid to him at the time he arrives at the age of Twenty one years old but in the event of my grandson Thomas Jacob Savage dying before he arrives at the age of Twenty one years old and leaving no child or issue lawfully begotten of his body at the time of his Death then and in that case I give the said Three Thousand heretofore given him to my children to be equally divided between them forever.

Item. I lend to my wife Catherine Savage the whole of my Estate during her lifetime or so long as she remains my widow except the Three Thousand dollars which I have given to my grandson Thomas Jacob Savage which she is to pay to him if she is living at the time he arrives to the age of Twenty one years old or leaves issue lawfully begotten of his body but in the event of her dying before my grandson Thos. J. Savage arrives at the age of Twenty one years old then my Will is that Lewis Heath should pay over to him the said Three Thousand Dollars when he should so arrive at that age. but in case my wife should get married in that event she is to take her one third part of my Estate during her life and the balance to go to my children as I hereafter devise.

Item. I give to my Son George Franklin the plantation I now live on called Westview to him and his heirs forever also that part of the land which I purchased from the Sheriff belonging to the Heirs of John H. Bayly which land was purchased to be divided between my son Sylvester H. Savage and myself also the money out of my Estate Sufficient to complete his education so long as he may wish to go to school to him and his Heirs forever.

Item. I give to my Daughter Emeline Susan Heath the plantation I purchased of the Sheriff belonging to the Heirs of William Dixon called Greenville, and also the sum of One Thousand Dollars to her and her Heirs forever.

Item. I Emancipate and Sett Free all my negroes at the following dates hereafter mentioned provided they Shall remove and leave the State of Virginia within Six months after they shall go free but if they do not remove and leave the State aforesaid within the six months then and in that case to become slaves to my Heirs forever and provided also that the laws of the State Shall _____ them to leave it.

Toby and Isaac	to go Free the 1st day of January 1840
Leah and Margaret	to go Free the 1st day of January 1842
Thamer and Charlotte	to go Free the 1st day of January 1844
Leah Church	to go Free the 1st day of January 1844
George and Catherine	to go Free the 1st day of January 1845

Tincey	to go Free the 1st day of January 1847
David and Lewis	to go Free the 1st day of January 1857
Jane	to go Free the 1st day of January 1850
Ann Ellen and Amy	to go Free the 1st day in January 1860
James Harry and Mary Ann	to go Free the 1st day in January 1862
John Joe and Harriet	to go Free the 1st day in January 1864
Marion and Rachel	to go Free the 1st day in January 1867
Jasper and Laura	to go Free the 1st day in January 1870
Newton and Bennet	to go Free the 1st day in January 1871

Item the issue or children that my Negroes may have during the time they may have to Serve shall belong to my Estate until they arrive at the age of Thirty years old and be equally between my children-

Item I give the remainder of my Estate not heretofore given including the Service of my negroes the time they have to serve to my three children George Franklin Savage Rosey Ann Savage and Emeline Susan Heath to be equally divided between them but if my Daughter Emeline Susan Heath should die leaving no child living at the time of her death then and in the case the Negroes that may go to her to return to my Estate to be divided between my two children, George Franklin Savage and Rosey Ann Savage to them and their Heirs forever.
I Nominate and appoint Lewis Heath and William A. Christian my Executors to this my last Will and Testament I witness whereof I have hereunto set my Hand Seal this the 27th day of June 1836.

Arthur R. Savage (SEAL)

In presents of
Wm A. Christian
George H. Young
John Andrews
James Savage

At a Court held for Northampton Count the 15th day of February 1837
This last will & testament of Arthur R. Savage deed was proved by the oaths of Wm A. Christian & James Savage, witnesses thereof, & ordered to be recorded. And on the motions of Wm. A. Christian & Lewis Heath, executors in the Said will named, who made oath & together with Robert S. Trower & John N. Brickhouse, their Securities, entered into & acknowledged a bond, according to law in the penalty of $20,000 certificate is granted the said Wm. A. Christian & Lewis Heath for obtaining a probate of the said will in due forever

Ex. Teste. N. J. Winder C.N.C.

THE WILL OF SIMON WILMER EMANCIPATING SYLVIA (SYLVA) WILMER, THE MOTHER OF MARY WILMER

In the name of God, Amen, I Simon Wilmer Rector of Christ Church and Chapel of St. John's Parish, Prince George and Charles Counties State of Mary., being in usual health and a sound and disposing mind and memory praised be god; -impressed with the shortness and uncertainty of life, as well as the impropriety of having anything important left undone, and wishing to have my house continually set in order not only constantly examining the State of my Soul, by settling my worldly affairs while I have Strength and capacity for the undertaking, do; in the presence of God and with a Knowledge of my responsibility to Him, make and publish this my Last will and testament, in manner and form following that is to say-

First and principally I commit my Soul into the hands of God my Saviour, who gave and redeemed it with his most precious blood, so that a poor Sinner may be justified in the name of the Lord Jesus, and Sanctified by the Spirit of only god-and also my body to be plainly entered, without any expression approbatory, or complimentary in a Sermon, obituary, epitaph, or otherwise; there; to rest until the morning of the resurrection, when Soul and body shall be united to praise the_____God forever-

Item, as the greater part of the estate was my wife's before our marriage, and with the hope that she will as a steward of the most High God make a proper distribution of the same, I will and bequeath to her the residue of my property, real, personal and mixed, with what may yet be acquired, to her and her heirs forever, subject to the following reservation, vizt. 1st-as it respects the colored people, it is my desire that those belonging to me in Virginia the children of Sylva shall serve until twenty five years old, the mother to be free immediately-and with respect to those formerly belonging to my wife, Harry, James, and Caroline on account of Costs and expenses should serve ten years from the date of this instrument- 2-dly from the sale of the Land, Seven Tracts containing about twenty four hundred acres in Pennsylvania (deeded jointly to Morgan Jones of Wilmington Delaware and myself) it is my will that on account of money paid to me by my Brother William deceased with an understanding that he should be interested with me although not named in the deed it is my will that his widow Ann B. Wilmer shall be entitled to one half of my part as soon as it can be sale be obtained 3dly It is my desire that my three Sons John Richard Frisby, Joseph R. B. and William L S beloved as they must ever be shall have my Books, and papers, as also my wearing apparel and shaving apparatus, with the exception of socks as may be desired by my wife, and that my Daughter Mary Ann Frisby shall have my silver coffee Pot, and state as an expression also of a Fathers affection.

4th- Should my wife die without a will, and have Children, or a child) yet unborn at date of this instrument, such part of the estate willed to her shall be divided among them if more than one, or if but one, a sum equal to what has been left to her other children by their Father, with the addition of a thousand dollars to each living to be twenty one years old-the balance to be divided between the American Bible society, the American Sunday School Union Society, the American Tract Society, the maryland Colonization Society and the American Temperance Society-

lastly, I hereby nominate constitute, and appoint my beloved wife Mary Eleanor sole executrix of this my last will and Testament, without requiring any securityship to the Court, and as the guardian of my children.

Signed, Sealed published and declared
by the same Simon Wilmer to be
his last will and Testament on the   Simon Wilmer {SEAL}
6th day of march in the year of our
Lord one thousand, Eight hundred and

thirty eight in the presence of us as
witnesses   Tho. I Marshall
                 Wm Marshall
                 John M. Brown
                 Peter Dent
Annexed to the foregoing will it is thus written
June Term 1840
Charles County Set, July 14th 1840, then came Mary Eleanor Wilmer Executrix of Simon Wilmer last of Charles county deceased and made Oath on the Holy Evangely of almighty god that the within and foregoing instrument of writing is the true and whole last will and testament of said deceased that hath come to her hands and possession and that she doth not know of any other.

Test Aquilla Bateman Regr. of wills Charles County set. July 14th 1840 then came Thomas Marshall, William Marshall, John, M. Brown and Peter Dent and subscribing witnesses to the within last will and testament of Simon Wilmer late of Charles County deceased and severally made Oath on the Holy Evangely of Almighty God that they did see the Testator there in named sign and seal this will, that they heard him publish pronounce and declare the same to be his last will and testament, and at the time of his so doing he was to the best of their apprehensions of sound and disposing mind memory and understanding and that they respectively subscribed their names as witnesses to this will in the presence and at the request of the Testator and in the presence of each other.
same to be his last will and testament, and at the time of his so doing he was to the best of their apprehensions of sound and disposing mind memory and understanding and that they respectively subscribed their names as witnesses to this will in the presence and at the request of the Testator and in the presence of each other.

                                                                Tes. Aquilla Bateman Regr. of Wills

THE WILL OF JOHN PITTS

I John Pitts of Northampton County make this my last will & testament first I give in trust with major S. Pitts and Arthur R. Savage all my slaves for a term of years hereafter expressed for them to be hired out & the hires to e hires to be divided between Anslo Dennis, & Edmund her son & Sally her daughter, & James her son, & one she is now pregnant with, the term for, Elijah, & Joshua & Minna to be hired is five years & at the expiration of that time I give them their freedom, & George & Rose, & Candis, to be hired out seven years & at the expiration of that time I give them their freedom & Nat, Adah, Mark, Isaac, Parker, Caleb, Toney, Esther, Leah, Sam & Bell, to be hired out until they arrive to the ages of twenty five years, & as they arrive to twenty five years old I give them their freedom, may old negroe man Toney I give his freedom and should he want aid my will is that he shall have it out of the hire of above named negroes as the trustees think he needs it, my will is that Edmond above named shall have all my wearing apparell & my sons, Item I give one hundred dollars each unto, Hezikiah Pitts, Major L. Pitts, Polly West, Ann Bailey & Sarah S. Pitts, Item I give unto Anslo Dennis one bed & furniture, my will is that all my estate except legacies shall be sold & after paying off the legacies the remainder to be divided between the above mentioned children of Anslo Dennis, I nominate and appoint, my friend and relation Major L. Pitts my executor of this my last will and testament Revoking all other wills heretofore made, witness my hand this third day of June 1816.

                                                                           John Pitts

Teste
Robert James, Preson Savage
     his
Henry X Dolby
     mark

At a Court held for Northampton County the 8th day of March 1819, this will & Codicil of John Pitts dec'd. were proved by the oath of Robert James a witness thereto & ordered recorded. And upon the motion of Major L. Pitts the executor therein appointed & he having taken the oath & entered into bond with security according to law certificate is granted the said Major L. Pitts of obtaining a probat thereof in due form.

                                                                    Teste
                                                                   Examd. B. Upshur C. N. C.

APPENDIX IV

DEFINITIONS OF LEGAL TERMS

Aid and abet	to actively, knowingly, intentionally, or purposefully facilitate or assist another individual in the commission or attempted commission of a crime
Alias execution	or else execution
Battery	the unlawful application of force to the person of another
Bequest	a gift of personal property contained in a will
Bona fide	in good faith; without fraud or deceit
Bond	written instrument with sureties, guaranteeing faithful performance of acts or duties contemplated
Chancery	that jurisprudence which is exercised in a court of equity
Clericus Curiae	Clerk of the Court
Defendant	in civil proceedings, the party responding to the complaint, in criminal proceeding, also called accused
De futuro	in the future
Divers	many, several, sundry, a grouping of unspecified persons, things, and acts
Enfeoff	to create a feoffment [early common law means of conveying freehold estate] Enfeoff has been used as a word granting title in some modern deeds
Et al /et allus	and another
Et alls/ et alli	and others
Et cetera (etc)	and other things
Et ux et uxor	conveyance by a man and his wife
Fee simple	outright ownership, with no restrictions
Felony	generic term employed to distinguish certain high crimes from minor offenses know as misdemeanors

Gaol	An early-American spelling of jail
Goods and chattel	any tangible, movable thing; personal, as opposed to real estate
Grand Jury	a body of people (generally 23 in number drawn, selected, and summoned according to law to serve. The purpose of the body is to investigate and inform on crimes and to indict them for crimes when there is sufficient evidence to warrant holding a person for trial
Ipso facto	a deed with no restrictions
Indictment	a formal written accusation, drawn up and submitted to a grand jury by the public prosecuting attorney
Justice	an officer of a county court
Larceny	the taking of another person's property unlawfully, with the intention of depriving the owner of its use. Grand and petit larceny refers to the value of that which is taken
Magistrate	a public civil official, invested with some part of the legislative, executive, or judicial power
Nihil dicit	he says nothing
Non est factum	it is not a fact
Non est inventus	he is not found
Notarius publicus	Notary public
Oyer	hearing. At common law, the reading to a defendant upon his demand the writ upon which the action is brought
Oyer and Terminer	in English law, special tribunals empowered to hear and determine cases within their criminal jurisdiction, commissioned by the King when the delay involved in ordinary prosecution count not be tolerated, as in the case of sudden insurrection
Plaintiff	one who files a law suit
Posthumous child	a child born after the death of the father
Poll	one qualified to vote

Polls	voting precincts
Quietus est	it is at rest
Recordat	it is recorded
Show cause order	an order [made upon the motion of one party] requiring a party to appear and show cause [argue] why a certain thing should not be done or permitted
Sic	in like manner
Summons	a mandate requiring the appearance of said defendant in said action under penalty of having judgement entered for failure to do so
Tenant by courtesy	the right of a man to hold property owned by a deceased wife for life when there are children to later own it
Test	witness
Tithable	a person who pays taxes
To wit	namely
True bill	same as indictment
Vizt.	namely

REFERENCES
BOOKS AND DOCUMENTS

Ames, Susie M., ed.,*County Court Records of Accomack-Northampton, Virginia 1640-1645*. Charlottesville: Virginia Historical Society, 1973.

Berlin, Ira, *Slaves Without Masters, The Free Negro in the Antebellum South*. New York: Pantheon Books,1941.

Black, Henry Campbell, *Blacks Law Dictionary*. 1968.

Gifis, Steven H., *Law Dictionary*. Barron's. 1984.

Grant, Joanne, *Black Protest, 1619 to the Present*. New York: Fawcett Premier, 1968.

Hening, William Waller, *Statutes At Large*. 1823.

Jackson, Luther P., *Free Negro Labor & Property Holding in Virginia, 1830-1860*. New York: 1969.

Katz, William L., *Black Indians, A Hidden Heritage*. New York: Ethrac Publications, 1986.

Mariner, Kirk. *Revival's Children, A Religious History of Virginia's Eastern Shore*. Salisbury: Peninsula Press 1979.

Mellon, James, *Bullwhip Days, The Slaves Remember*. New York: Avon Books,1988.

Mihalyka, Jean, *Marriages Northampton County, Virginia 1660/1-1854*. Bowie: Heritage Books, 1990.

Northampton County Order Book 40, 1837-1841.

Northampton County Order Book 44, 1857-1865.

Register of Free Negroes, Northampton County, Virginia (1853-1861). Original Manuscript-Clerk's Office, Eastville, Virginia.

Russell, John H., *The Free Negro in Virginia-1619-1865*. New York: Dover Publications, 1969.

Whitelaw, Ralph T. *Virginia's Eastern Shore*. Richmond: Virginia Historical Society, 1951. 2 vol.

United States Census, Northampton County, 1790.

United States Census, Northampton County, 1810.

United States Census, Northampton County, 1820.

United States Census, Northampton County, 1830.

United States Census, Northampton County, 1840.

United States Census, Northampton County, 1850.

INDEX OF FREE NEGROES

NAME	NO.	PAGE	NAME	NO.	PAGE	NAME	NO.	PAGE
Aims, John	125	18	Church, Abel	176	26	Collins, Caleb	11	2
Ames, John Jr.	192	28	Church, Abel Jr	86	12	Cotrell, Elizabeth Sr	166	24
Ames, Mahala	54	8	Church, Abel Jr.	289	42	Cottrel, Peggy	134	19
Ames, Mary	287	42	Church, Elizabeth	28	4	Cottrell, Dennis	263	39
Anthony, Jane	25	4	Church, Jacob	235	35	Cottrell, Elizabeth	155	22
Anthony, Pricilla	10	2	Church, James	22	4	Cottrell, Emeline	246	36
Becket, Bethany	178	26	Church, James	168	24	Cottrell, James	154	22
Becket, Elizabeth	214	32	Church, Leah	200	29	Cottrell, Jeptha	153	22
Becket, Jane	228	34	Church, Littleton	52	8	Drighouse, Bridget	212	31
Becket, John	95	14	Church, Littleton	119	17	Drighouse, Nathan	98	14
Becket, John of Abram	217	32	Church, Littleton	236	35	Drighouse, William	183	27
			Church, Lucy	43	6	Fisher, Lewis	101	15
Becket, Keziah	156	22	Church, Mary	177	26	Francis, Abel	21	3
Becket, Leah	216	32	Church, Mary Ann	291	42	Francis, Abel	258	38
Becket, Margaret	215	32	Church, Solomon	229	34	Francis, Edna	279	41
Becket, Matilda	97	14	Churches, Nelson	244	36	Francis, Horace	30	5
Becket, Peter	163	24	Collins, Adah	23	4	Francis, Polly	13	2
Becket, William of Rachel	243	36	Collins, Adah N.	88	13	Francis, Polly	259	38
			Collins, Alfred	109	16	Francis, Sabra	20	3
Becket, Wm	160	23	Collins, Ann	81	12	Francis, Sally	260	38
Bevans, Elizabeth	57	8	Collins, Ann	202	30	Francis, Wesley	278	41
Bevans, Emeline	142	21	Collins, Ann	241	36	Giddens, Daniel	172	25
Bevans, Esther	59	9	Collins, Ann Eliza	108	16	Giddens, Esther	184	27
Bevans, Joseph	56	8	Collins, Caleb	282	41	Giddens, Henry	121	17
Bevans, Matilda	231	34	Collins, Christopher	270	40	Giddens, James	73	10
Bevans, Robert	143	21	Collins, Elizabeth	196	29	Giddens, Sally	64	9
Bevans, Samuel	230	34	Collins, Elizabeth S.	87	12	Gleason, Peter	195	29
Bevans, Shadrack	133	19	Collins, Emma	137	20	Gleeson, Margaret	34	5
Brickhouse, Bridget	69	10	Collins, Esther	51	8	Griffin, Sophia	67	10
Brickhouse, Caroline	70	10	Collins, Esther	248	37	Guy, Mary	232	34
Brickhouse, Drucilla	66	10	Collins, Fannie	159	23	Harman, James	211	31
Brickhouse, Elizabeth	79	11	Collins, Griffin Jr	205	30	Harmon, Laura	210	31
Brickhouse, Ellen	213	32	Collins, Henry	60	9	Harmon, Margaret	284	42
Brickhouse, Emily	63	9	Collins, Henry	115	17	Harmon, William Edw.	18	3
Brickhouse, Jack	93	13	Collins, Henry	290	42	Heath, David	102	15
Brickhouse, Johnson	14	2	Collins, Jacob	17	3	Howell, Custis	268	39
Brickhouse, Leah	281	41	Collins, Jacob	151	22	Howell, John	139	20
Brickhouse, Margaret	292	42	Collins, James	104	15	Howell, Rachel	201	30
Brickhouse, Mary Ann	75	11	Collins, James E.	84	12	Howell, William	174	25
Brickhouse, Peggy	132	19	Collins, Lavinia	147	21	Jacob, Emeline	233	34
Brickhouse, Rachel	65	9	Collins, Louisa	169	24	Jacob, Lloyd Wm.	264	39
Brickhouse, Smith	92	13	Collins, Margaret	55	8	Johnson, Elizabeth	58	8
Brickhouse, Tabitha	113	16	Collins, Maria	204	30	Johnson, John	99	14
Brickhouse, Wesley	118	17	Collins, Maria A.	148	21	Johnson, Levin	110	16
Brickhouse, William	78	11	Collins, Mary Ann	136	20	Johnson, Michael	72	10
Brickhouse, William	262	39	Collins, Mary Jane	82	12	Jubilee, Susy	112	16
Burton, George	180	26	Collins, Noah	138	20	Kendall, Isaac	221	33
Burton, Mary	181	26	Collins, Ralph	103	15	Lecato, George	24	4
Carter, Samuel	8	2	Collins, Roxaline	249	37	Lecato, George	123	18
Carter, Samuel	175	25	Collins, Sabra	283	42	Lecato, Jacob	120	17
Carter, Tamer	158	23	Collins, Sarah	203	30	Lecato, Jane	122	18
Carter, William	46	7	Collins, Smith	96	14	Lecato, William	107	15
Catt, Mary A.	240	35	Collins, Susan	245	36	Matthews, Damary	209	31
Catt, Sabra B.	239	35	Collins, Vianna	152	22	Matthews, Levi	68	10
Christian, Elizabeth	39	6	Collins, Victor C.	274	40	Matthews, Mary	250	37

NAME	NO.	PAGE
Matthews, Solomon	223	33
Morris, Custis	271	40
Morris, Francis Asberry	276	41
Morris, Henry	36	5
Morris, Henry Jr.	50	7
Morris, John	26	4
Morris, Mary	186	27
Morris, Michael	27	4
Morris, Smith	130	19
Morris, Stockely	280	41
Moses, Esther	150	22
Moses, Frederick	149	21
Moses, Levin	220	33
Moses, Maria	165	24
Moses, Ned	91	13
Onley, John Wesley	207	31
Onley, William	226	33
Only, Michael	89	13
Pool, Henry	90	13
Perkins, Esther	61	9
Pitts, Belle	188	27
Pitts, Esther	257	38
Pitts, Leah	191	28
Pitts, William	114	16
Pool, Charles	127	18
Pool, Joseph	4	1
Pool, Joseph	131	19
Pool, Nancy	116	17
Poulson, Betsy	117	17
Poulson, Esther	179	26
Poulson, George	275	40
Poulson, Rachel	45	7
Reed, Ann	144	21
Reed, George	40	6
Reed, Horace	41	6
Reed, Isaac	252	37
Reid, John	129	19
Roan, Mary	182	26
Roan, Michael	94	13
Rozell, Betsy	277	41
Rozell, Emily	128	18
Rozell, Lewis	106	15
Rozell, Louisa	234	35
Rozell, Mary	1	1
Rozell, Sabra	2	1
Rozell, Sarah	7	1
Rozelle, James	251	37
Satchell, Agnes	140	20
Satchell, Ann	47	7
Satchell, John	48	7
Satchell, John	100	14
Satchell, Mary	9	2
Satchell, Mary Ann	29	5
Satchell, Peggy	141	20
Satchell, Peter	35	5
Satchell, Robert	38	6
Satchell, Smith	37	6
Savage, Amy	238	35
Savage, Geraldine	124	18
Savage, Isaac	6	1
Savage, Tobey	3	1
Scisco, Harriet	266	39
Scisco, Henry	267	39
Simkins, George	265	39
Simkins, George Avery	256	38
Simkins, Joshua	193	28
Simkins, Sally Ann	254	37
Simkins, Tamar	83	12
Simkins, Tamar	255	38
Sisco, Wm. Henry	135	19
Spady, Jim	42	6
Stephens, Amy	16	3
Stephens, Amy	194	28
Stephens, Arinthia	261	39
Stephens, Arthur	71	10
Stephens, Burley	167	24
Stephens, Chapman	126	18
Stephens, Dinah	198	29
Stephens, Elizabeth	189	28
Stephens, George	44	7
Stephens, George	80	11
Stephens, George	293	42
Stephens, Jack	162	23
Stephens, John	31	5
Stephens, John	272	40
Stephens, Joseph	32	5
Stephens, Kitty	219	32
Stephens, Margaret	146	21
Stephens, Margaret Jr	197	29
Stephens, Mary	53	8
Stephens, Mary	269	40
Stephens, Mary Ann	190	28
Stephens, Mary Ann	247	36
Stephens, Patience	218	32
Stephens, Rosena	12	2
Stephens, Susan	161	23
Stephens, Wesley	105	15
Stephens, William	227	34
Stevens, Abram	206	30
Stevens, John	74	11
Stevens, Rachel	145	21
Stevens, Severn	237	35
Stockley, Ann	157	23
Sutton, Nathaniel	33	5
Sutton, Nathaniel	253	37
Thompson, Louisa	225	33
Trower, Luke	222	33
Upshur, John	273	40
Upshur, Joseph	5	1
Upshur, Joseph	111	16
Upshur, Louisa	15	3
Upshur, Mary	199	29
Wallace, William	19	3
Webb, Henry	208	31
Webb, James	62	9
Webb, John	85	12
Webb, William	288	42
Weeks, Edward	170	25
Weeks, Elizabeth	76	11
Weeks, Esther	173	25
Weeks, Frances Sarah	286	42
Weeks, George	185	27
Weeks, Lavinia	171	25
Weeks, Lavinia Ellen	285	42
Weeks, Maria J.	242	36
Weeks, Mary	164	24
Weeks, Susan	77	11
White, Leah	187	27
Williams, Henrietta	224	33
Wilmer, Mary	49	7

NOTES

NOTES

www.ingramcontent.com/pod-product-compliance
Lightning Source LLC
Chambersburg PA
CBHW080252170426
43192CB00014BA/2647